Clutter
Junkie
No More

Stepping Up to Recovery

Clutter Junkie
No More

Barb Rogers

Conari
Press

First published in 2007 by Conari Press,
an imprint of Red Wheel/Weiser, LLC
With offices at:
500 Third Street, Suite 230
San Francisco, CA 94107
www.redwheelweiser.com

ISBN 10: 1–57324–288–8
ISBN 13: 978–1–57324–288–2

Library of Congress Cataloging-in-Publication Data
Rogers, Barb, 1947–
    Clutter junkie no more : stepping up to recovery / Barb Rogers.
        p. cm.
    ISBN 1-57324-288-8 (alk. paper)
    1. Simplicity—Religious aspects.   2. Self-help techniques.
    3. Twelve-step programs.   I. Title.
    BJ1496.R64   2007
    648'.8—dc22   2006021361

Cover and text design by rlf design
Typeset in Dante MT

Printed in Canada
TCP
10 9 8 7 6 5 4 3 2 1

I would like to dedicate this book to my friend

Donna Gordon. Donna, you were my inspiration and my

angel with research. My life would have a great empty spot if

it weren't for you and your fur babies, Nikki and Calvin.

My love and thanks for everything.

Contents

Acknowledgments

To my husband, Tommy Rogers, Jr., who is my rock. You truly know what it is to give unconditional love, and show it in so many ways. Thank you for helping my dreams come true. I will love you forever.

To my dogs, Georgie and Sammi, who love me even when I'm at my worst. You have brought me so much joy and filled my heart with love.

To my family, friends, and those friends of Bill who have loved and supported me in all my endeavors. You are always in my mind and my heart.

The Twelve Steps
of Clutterers Anonymous

1. We admitted we were powerless over clutter, that our lives had become unmanageable.

2. Came to believe that a power greater than ourselves could restore us to sanity.

3. Made a decision to turn our will and our lives over to the care of God as we understood God.

4. Made a searching and fearless moral inventory of ourselves.

5. Admitted to God, to ourselves, and to another human being the exact nature of our wrongs.

6. Were entirely ready to have God remove all these defects of character.

7. Humbly asked God to remove our shortcomings.

8. Made a list of all persons we had harmed, and became willing to make amends to them all.

9. Made direct amends to such people wherever possible, except when to do so would injure them or others.

10. Continued to take personal inventory and when we were wrong, promptly admitted it.

11. Sought through prayer and meditation to improve our conscious contact with God, as we understood God, praying only for the knowledge of God's will for us and the power to carry that out.

12. Having had a spiritual awakening as a result of these steps, we tried to carry this message to others, and to practice these principles in all our affairs.

(Adapted from Alcoholics Anonymous)

The Clutter Junkie

"I'm overwhelmed," is the daily cry of true clutter junkies, everywhere. Shame and despair haunt their days as they wonder why they aren't like other people. They believe that some day, some way, if they could just get their mess cleaned up, the problem would be solved . . . they would be "normal." Life becomes a treadmill of purchasing organizational materials, hiring a cleaning person, or taking an entire week and nearly working themselves to death, only to realize within a short time, they are right back where they started.

Other people, who don't suffer from an addiction to clutter, do not understand. Judgments can be harsh. Why can't they just clean up their mess? Are they lazy? How hard can it be? The rest of us clean up our own messes. How can they live like that? In truth, such people might as well say to an alcoholic, "Why don't you just stop drinking?" Don't you think they would if they could? Like any other addiction, the clutter is but a symptom of underlying problems.

People with eating disorders are seeking control in a world they consider out of their control. The alcoholic and drug addict escape reality and feelings by altering their minds. Gambling addicts escape life problems as they sit mesmerized by gambling machines, cards, lottery tickets, waiting for the rush of winning. What is the payoff for the clutter junkie? As long as they remain overwhelmed, they don't have to live life, move forward, and they always have an excuse.

Many clutter junkies will take on extra work, volunteer for nonprofit organizations, go out of their way to do for others, to avoid their problem, to have an excuse for staying overwhelmed. They believe they will feel better about not getting their mess cleaned up if they have a good reason. However, that is just a Band-Aid on a gushing wound.

Clutter is a wall constructed bit by bit to keep the world out. However, as with other addictions, it becomes the prison that keeps the addict in. Therefore, in looking for a solution to clutter addiction, the addict must take the wall down bit by bit. It didn't get built overnight, and it won't go away overnight. It will take time. It will take a conscious effort. It will take walking through the fear that keeps the clutter junkie's life a mess.

The Nesting Syndrome

For over twenty years, while in recovery from my own addictions, I've had the opportunity to work with others. I discovered that many addicts have a tendency to move from one addiction to another in a futile effort to fill those holes in themselves that brought them to addiction in the first place. One of those holes is the feeling of helplessness and being out of control of their lives. The new addiction takes them back to a more comfortable place . . . a place where they feel at least in control of one thing in their life, even if it's unhealthy.

One woman, who I know well, even after twenty years of recovery from alcoholism, experienced a traumatic event that would forever change her life. She knew she couldn't drink, feared drug addiction, but her life was spiraling out of control. The addict inside cried out for control. And so the shopping began, and was soon followed by clutter. Within a few months, this lovely woman, a person who had elegant dinner parties at her house, who loved to entertain, built a nest at the end of her couch, surrounded by a wall of clutter that kept others, and the world, out. She felt safe.

Nesting is a common habit of clutter addicts. It doesn't matter if it's one end of the couch, a special comfortable chair, or a cleared-off spot on the bed. It's that safe place they go when they are in avoidance, or fear, of life and problems.

Like the gambler who is drawn back to the same gambling machine or poker table, the alcoholic who returns over and over to the same bar, the same stool, or the overeater who has a special place to stash their comfort food, the clutterer will return to the nest. Everything they need is close at hand: the telephone, snacks, tissues, an ashtray, the television remote, a place to set their drink. Hours may pass as they ponder what they want to get done, how they will go about it, or what they need to purchase to help them get organized.

Many clutterers are obsessed with books, tapes, and television shows about how to get organized, how to decorate their living spaces. They may even order many gadgets to make it easier, only to discover that the gadgets don't work for them. The gadgets, tapes, and books simply become a part of the clutter wall. While still in avoidance, they tell themselves the darn thing just didn't work.

Sitting in their nests, they might consider their surroundings. Maybe if they bought something new, or different, it would help. Which brings us to another thing clutter addicts have in common: they seek out distractions. They can spend an entire day, in the midst of their chaos, trying to figure out where, and how, to hang that new painting, or place the new lamp, or a chair, in the perfect spot. It doesn't help. Again, in a very short time, the new item becomes a part of the clutter wall. They find themselves back at that old familiar place, feeling helpless, hopeless, their mind screaming, "I'm overwhelmed!" Back to the nest.

There are people who think there is a simple solution to the nesting syndrome. Believe me when I tell you that it does not help to remove the nest, move the furniture around, even to gut the living space and start over. True clutter addicts will rebuild their wall over and over until they accept the fact that they have a problem, and put a name to it, and admit that their addiction is affecting every facet of their life. The clutter wall, the nest, can only be disassembled by the person who built it.

All addictions are based in fear and are used for avoidance. Fear of other people, an inability to trust, self-esteem issues, and the feeling of not fitting into the world around them is what draws the clutter addict to things and, in many cases, pets. Animals expect nothing, do not judge, and give unconditional love. They are safe. Possessions will never betray us. Even if they break, they can be replaced—unlike human beings. The clutter addict believes their need for love and acceptance can be filled by pets, and that if they have enough stuff, they can build their own little world where others and situations can't get through the clutter to them . . . to the person they believe isn't good enough. They don't realize that there will never be enough stuff, and, no matter how wonderful the animals are and how much they are loved, they can not replace the feelings between two human beings. Fido has simply entered the nest, which enables the clutter addict to spend even more time there.

Unlike the drunk, who acts out when drinking, or a person with an eating disorder, whose problem shows through gain or loss of weight, the clutter addict's appearance can be deceiving. Many are obsessed with looking good. It becomes terribly important to make a good impression on the outside world. Hours may be spent daily on grooming, picking out the right thing to wear, even if it's just to go the grocery store or the post office.

Because of this obsession, the clutter addict may spend a great deal of time and money shopping, until shopping becomes a peripheral addiction. As a secondary addiction, shopping fills two needs. It's a distraction, and it enables the addict to hide their clutter addiction from the world. If they look okay, they must be okay. However, no matter how good they can make themselves look on the outside, inside the clutter lives on, not only in their house, but in their mind. When the day is done, they return to the nest.

As they spiral out of control with their shopping and clutter problem, finances can become an issue. Like the drug addict who needs to feed his habit, eventually, clutter addicts will use money geared for essentials to feed the addiction. Buying is a quick fix. The fix wears off, and they soon need another one. Maybe they could make the car payment late. The late fee isn't that much. They'll catch up next month. But, like the clutter, the spiraling bills begin to grow until they find themselves back in the nest, their mind crying, "I'm overwhelmed. What am I going to do?"

Before admitting to the problem, the addiction, the clutter addict might try several other methods. They are ripe for organizations that promise to consolidate their bills, cut down their interest payments, give them equity loans on their home, even look into the possibility of bankruptcy. Bankruptcy is a difficult scenario for them to accept. If they do that, if anyone finds out, it could ruin the image they've worked so hard on. Sometimes it comes to that, and they find a way through it. Lots of people declare bankruptcy. They tell themselves it's not like it used to be. People don't look down on it as they did in the past.

A fresh start. They'll do better this time. Usually, for a while, they do. They might make out a budget, buy an organizer, a new book on how to deal with finances better, or even get a financial advisor. As with every other addiction, as long as they don't look at the problem, admit they have a problem, sooner or later, the addiction will rear its ugly head again. . . . It will become a vicious cycle of problems, quick fixes, delusions, and keeping up appearances.

What does it take for a clutter addict to hit bottom? Some simply get sick and tired of being sick and tired and living the way they are. Others have to lose everything before becoming willing to admit the problem. It doesn't matter how they come to the realization of their clutter addiction, as much as it does what they do with it.

Many clutter addicts, like other addicts, are misdiagnosed by mental health care professionals. "Depressed, just depression," the doctor said. "Take this pill. It will help." Pills may help, but they will not resolve the underlying problems that will continually bring the addict back to the addiction. When the pill doesn't work, the clutter addict will experience those old feelings of not being good enough, of failure, the same early feelings that put them on the road to addiction.

Although there may be other solutions, by far the most effective solution I've seen is a twelve-step program used by so many other addicts. There is something to be said for dealing with other people who have the same problem as you. They understand. They don't judge. Since they have been down the same road, no explanations are necessary. It's a safe place where clutter addicts can be honest, not only with others, but with themselves. The program is anonymous; the clutter addict can protect that so-important image until they realize that they can become what they want the world to believe they are.

A twelve-step program is not a quick fix. It is a lifelong process played out one day at a time. The first step helps the clutter addict understand there is a problem, a real addiction that is just as serious as any other addiction. The addict is not alone, as many others suffer from the same addiction. The next two steps take the clutter addict to a spirituality by introducing him or her to a God of their understanding, a God that they can live with that will nurture and help them in all their endeavors, and understand that they are imperfect human beings.

Steps 4 through 9 are the action steps. It will take time, it will take effort, it will take daily persistence to work these steps. However, the clutter addict has their whole life to do it. It's better to take the time to do the steps fully and completely. What you get from them depends on what you put into them.

Through the action steps, clarity will emerge. An understanding will arise of why they have lived the way they have, of what brought them to that point, and what specific things they can do to change not only their behavior, but their way of thinking. These are a guide to resolutions of the past, a way to live in the present, and to find one's place in the world.

The last three steps help clutter addicts to maintain a new way of life. Certain things can be done on a daily basis that allow the addict to live a better life. They remind clutter addicts every day what needs to be done so that they don't slip back into an old way of thinking, an old way of living.

Clutter
Junkie
No More

Stepping Up to Recovery

*We admitted we were powerless over clutter,
that our lives had become unmanageable.*

STEP 1, "We admitted we were powerless over clutter, that our lives had become unmanageable," speaks of several things. The first word, *we,* tells us we are not alone. We are not crazy. There are others like us. There is a lot of relief in knowing we are not the only one out there living with the problem.

The admission of powerlessness doesn't make us weak. There are many things in life that we are powerless over. When we are physically ill, we turn our power over to doctors. Legal problems compel us to turn our power over to attorneys and judges. Accountants, banks, and financial advisors are empowered by their education to deal with our financial situations. It's wise to turn over our power to those who can help, who can use their knowledge to guide us.

Once the line is crossed into addiction, the choice to clutter or not to clutter is not within your power. Think back to all the things you've done to try to control the clutter addiction. They didn't work because the clutter itself is simply a manifestation of what is happening within you.

How is your life affected by clutter? Perhaps you'd like to have people in, but can't because you don't want them to see your mess. It's difficult to have friends, intimate relationships, if shame keeps you from letting anyone in. Therefore, most of your relationships must be kept on a superficial level. You can tell yourself it's about the clutter in your house, but in reality, it is fear of intimacy, of allowing anyone to know who you really are. The outside clutter is an excuse, a barrier to keep others from getting too close.

Do you have trouble looking at yourself in the mirror? Do you look into your eyes, or focus on hair, skin, teeth, and the shape of your nose? If your eyes meet in the mirror, do you quickly look away and fumble around the numerous bottles around the sink to find that new product you bought last week to take care of those troubling wrinkles? If you understand what I mean, if you've done that, you know what it is not even to be able to have an intimate relationship with yourself. If you look any deeper than your skin, you might not like what you see.

Distractions are the great enabler of the clutter addict. As long as there is always an overwhelming number of things that need done, if importance is put on the outside of the body, the needs of pets, and so many other things, the days will pass, and the problems will be avoided yet again.

What about those days that are passing you by as you scramble toward one distraction after another, always keeping up appearances, protecting yourself from others and the world around you? If you're sitting in your nest, thinking about how overwhelmed you are, do you ever wonder about finding a solution, a new way to live?

There is a solution, and the first step is to understand that you suffer from clutter addiction, and it is making your life unmanageable. You are not inept, stupid, lazy, or all that different from other people. If you attended an anonymous meeting, you would see great similarities between yourself and the others in attendance. Addiction may show itself in different forms, but the feelings are the same. The most common feeling is that of not being good enough, not fitting in. We may tell ourselves our addiction makes us feel better, but the truth is that it sets us apart, feeds our poor self-esteem, and makes our world smaller and smaller, until we feel as if we are living in a box.

Admitting we have a problem, and the effect it is having on our life, is like opening the lid to the box. With that one conscious decision, we feel that first ray of sunshine, that warmth, that tells us there is hope.

If you're having trouble deciding whether you are truly a clutter addict, or just a messy person, there's a way to find out. The following questions will reveal the truth if you are willing to answer them with brutal honesty. It's okay to be honest because no one will see them, but you.

- Do you awaken filled with anticipation, or dread of the day ahead?

- Do past issues continually come up in dreams and thoughts?

- Do you feel tired a great deal of the time?

- Do you imagine illnesses to explain feeling tired?

- Do you obsess over your outward appearance?

- Do you have trouble setting reasonable goals and sticking to them?

- Do you finish one project before beginning another?

- When is the last time you invited someone into your home, a new person into your life?

- Do you continually make excuses for your mess, for who you are?

- Do you qualify your opinions by prefacing them with explanations and excuses?

- Do you compare yourself with what you believe others are?

- Do you have trouble accepting compliments?

- Is there anyone you trust completely?

- Do you volunteer, and do for others, at the expense of your own needs?

- Do you replace intimacy with people by loving pets, plants, and things?

- Do you have a nest?

- How much time is spent in the nest?

- Do you watch home improvement and decorating shows, and read magazines, and wish you were able to live like that?

- Do you buy impulsively, shop for the sake of shopping?

- Do you have trouble making decisions?

- Do you keep your finances in order?

- Where does your money go?

- When a problem arises, do you immediately go to the worst case scenario? Do you know serenity, peace, or is your mind as chaotic as your living space?

These are a few questions that will give you insight into whether you have crossed the line into clutter addiction. After considering them, answer the one question there is no escape from: Do you feel overwhelmed most of the time?

Life can be fascinating, frustrating, intriguing, even frightening at times. However, the one thing it shouldn't

be is overwhelming. As human beings, we have been endowed with all the tools required to deal with life, and
whatever it throws at us.

You might be thinking that it is easy for me to say, as
I sit in my nice house, writing my little books. But I know
overwhelmed. I lived overwhelmed until life became too
much to handle. By age thirty, I'd outlived all my children,
could not maintain relationships with family, friends, or
spouses, had spent time in a mental hospital, and desperately sought relief through addictions. I thought I wanted
to die.

When push came to shove, I didn't want to die. I just
wanted to find a better way to live. That way revealed itself to me in a twelve-step program. I became a part of
the "we." Living in the solution, instead of the problem,
began with that first step. I had a problem. I was powerless over it. I needed help.

Little did I know, when I took that first step, I would
be embarking on a journey to a life I couldn't have even
imagined. I thought if it gave me some relief, if I could
overcome that overwhelmed feeling, that would be
enough. However, it gave me so much more.

Although many years have passed since that first day,
my first meeting, it will be a day that stands out in my
life forever. Through that beginning, that first glimmer

of hope, I emerged from being what many considered as a hopeless case to a happy, productive member of the human race. I belong to the world, and it belongs to me.

If you are sitting in your nest, surrounded by clutter, your mind saying, "I'm overwhelmed," I hope you will think of me, and so many others like me, who have lived through the same struggle and found a way out. It begins with one step, admitting it is a problem, that you need help.

The Meeting

What about these meetings? What do people do there? Do the meetings really help? Why are they anonymous? Can steps for drunks and drug addicts really work for clutter addicts? Is it a religious thing? Where do I find these groups? These are some questions that might go through your mind when considering Clutterers Anonymous.

It may be amazing to think that where doctors, other professionals, clergy have failed, that one drunk helping another worked. These drunks, in recovery, then came up with twelve steps and twelve traditions to help guide them to a better way of life, to recovery from addiction. It spread worldwide. Next came the realization that if these things worked for drunks, they might work for drug addicts, people with eating disorders, gamblers, smokers, and more recently, clutterers.

The twelve-step program is based on the idea that no one can understand the compulsion the addict deals with better than someone who has felt it, known it, lived it, and found a way out. Compulsion is not the same as making a choice. Compulsion is an irresistible impulse to perform an irrational act. In other words, we keep doing it even when we don't want to do it. We don't believe we can stop.

In and of ourselves, we probably can't. But there is a way, and we find this out when we attend a meeting or meet online with others who have the same problem. They have discovered the way out, and are willing to share their experience, strength, and hope. They understand. The situations that brought each of you to the point of seeking help may have been different, but I guarantee the same feelings were involved. You have dealt with the same frustrations, fears, feelings of helplessness and hopelessness.

How is a meeting run? A group of people, all suffering from the same addiction, gather in a specific place. It can be an office, a coffee shop, a church basement, even a room online. There are discussion meetings in which one person offers up a topic, or problem, they've been having or thinking about, and one by one, others share about going through the same thing, how they got through it, and make suggestions the other person might try.

There are step meetings that concentrate on a different step each week . . . and sometimes the traditions, and participants speak of how they came to the step, worked through it, and came out on the other side. These meetings help give clarity to the twelve suggested steps and traditions of the meetings. They also show the newcomer that there are many different ways to work the steps, and that they have a choice of when and how to do what works for them.

There are speaker meetings. At a speaker meeting, one individual gets up and shares their story with the group. I've heard it said that if you stick around long enough, and listen, you will eventually hear your story. In hearing your story, or even parts of it, you come to understand you are not crazy. It really is an addiction, and you are not alone.

Although it is different in certain areas, most meetings begin with the Serenity Prayer and end with the Lord's Prayer, or vice versa. The steps and traditions are read aloud, and the meeting begins. You have a choice to speak or not speak, participate in the prayers, or not. You have a choice in everything you do, or choose not to do. I will say, however, that usually what you get out of a meeting is in direct correlation to what you are willing to put into it.

Over the years, I have seen the difference between those who simply attend meetings and those who have chosen to become a part of the group. Like all other addicts, the clutter addict has a problem with commitment, and this will be a big commitment. A twelve-step program is about changing every facet of your life. Only the first step mentions clutter; the other eleven tells us how to live an uncluttered life.

Anonymity serves several purposes. Some people do not wish the world to know they live the way they do. Others feel shame that they are addicted to anything and have had to ask for help. One of the most important facets of anonymity in a twelve-step meeting is that for that one hour, in that one moment, we are all the same. It doesn't matter if you are a doctor or waitress, whether you live in a mansion or a trailer, what religion, race, or economic level you come from. We are all just Sally, Joe, Betty, John, and we have a common problem.

Since addiction is no respecter of age, race, gender, or profession, addicts come from all walks of life, and from every religion, some with no beliefs at all. There-fore, religion has no place in a twelve-step meeting. We speak of a "God of our understanding," or a "Higher Power," which can be translated into whatever it is we each believe in.

In a meeting, at some point, a basket is passed for a contribution to help pay for coffee, snacks, and rent for the meeting place. Again, you have a choice. There are no dues or fees, but the groups are self-supporting. They do not accept outside money, so that there is no pres-sure on the group to conform to anyone else's ideas of what should be happening.

Does it work? People may fail to work the program, but if worked, the program never fails. I can see no way of implementing the twelve steps and traditions into your life and not coming out better off. The twelve steps and traditions give us direction, a plan of action, take away all our excuses and justifications for self-destructive be-havior, and tell us that we have a choice in all things. The people aren't the program, but the support of others like us can make the difference when we need that help-ing hand to get us through the moment. And, one day, when we become more sound, we become that helping hand that gets another addict through a crisis. And, they will help someone, and they will help someone, and that's how it works.

Get in touch with Clutterers Anonymous by going online to *http://www.clutterersanonymous.net* to find online meetings or to get a meeting list by region and date.

The Power of Two

*Came to believe that a power greater than
ourselves could restore us to sanity.*

Step 2, "Came to believe that a power greater than
ourselves could restore us to sanity," speaks to us
not about being insane in the usual sense, but about the
insanity of addiction. If you put twenty clutter addicts
in a room with other people, you wouldn't be able to
pick them out. They wouldn't be falling down drunk,
twitching, talking to themselves, wearing tin foil hats,
or picking imaginary flowers.

The insanity of addiction can be explained by the three "D's": denial, delusion, and deception. For the clutter addict, they go something like this.

Denial

It's not that bad. I could have this all put away, cleaned up, organized, in a couple of days if I just had the time. I don't know how my friend lives the way she does. She must spend all her time cleaning up stuff. I have a life, have things to do, people to see, more important things to think about than a few messes. I will get to it tomorrow, next week, next year, eventually. It's not that bad.

A person who doesn't have an addiction problem doesn't wonder if they do. It never crosses their mind. They don't spend their time searching for excuses, justifications, and rationalizations for their actions or lack of action. It doesn't matter what you are telling the rest of the world. However, what you tell yourself can make all the difference. As long as you can deny clutter is a problem, that it is actually an addiction, you can deny there is a reason for it in your life. The truth is that no matter how long you can use this avoidance technique, it won't make the problem go away. Just because you deny it doesn't mean it's not real.

Delusion

It's not affecting my life. I have friends. People who really care for me won't care what my house looks like. I don't care what people think anyway. I could live like them if I wanted to. This is just a matter of choices. There is so much going on in my life, I don't have time for unimportant tasks that simply have to be repeated every day to keep up with them. I make up for my clutter by helping others, volunteering at hospice, the library, taking care of my pets, my flowers, baby-sitting the neighbor's kids. I have a full and interesting life. What more could there be?

I call this the "run and hide" technique for avoidance. The clutter addict tends either to run as fast as they can, moving so quickly that no one can catch up with them, pin them down, or have an intimate relationship with them. Or, they hide behind that big wall of clutter, not allowing anyone inside. The few individuals who are allowed into their life spend a great deal of time under scrutiny, always feeling they have to prove their loyalty and that they can be trusted. Even then, it is difficult for the clutter addict to truly trust another person. If a person gets too close, begins to chip away at the wall, panic can set in. It's time to go shopping, find some more stuff to reinforce the wall, to let that person know there are serious boundaries that cannot be crossed. Therefore, relationships are kept on a superficial level, and all the while, clutter addicts tell themselves how deep and wonderful their relationships are.

Deception

Somehow, some way, some day, it will all change. I will just wake up one morning, clean up my mess, and I will be like other people. There is no big reason behind all this. I've been busy, tired, distracted, and have probably let it get a bit out of control, but I can fix it. I do need all this stuff. I know what I have, why I bought it, why I'm keeping it. I can do all those things other people can. It's simply a bit more difficult for me. Maybe it's a genetic thing, something my parents taught me, or I'm more sensitive than others. Whatever it is, and I'm sure it's not an addiction, I'm certain I can overcome it and control it. I should be able to control it.

Should? According to whom? As much as the clutter addict wants to believe it doesn't matter what others think, how they are judged, they spend a great deal of time comparing themselves to others. Considering how important it is for them to put on a good face in public, to make others think that they are okay when their life is in chaos, it seems to be difficult for them to understand that other people are doing the same thing. So, they compare their insides with other people's outsides, and always come up short. As long as they can continue to do that, they have an excuse to live in their deception that they are different from others, special in some way, and that excuses the addiction. So, the "should" is according to them.

Do you wonder if you can accept a power greater than yourself? If you think there is no power greater than yourself, stand in the doorway of your living space and look around. The power greater than yourself at that moment is your addiction to clutter. Think of all the things you've tried that didn't work. Have you given it your best effort? Yet, it is still there, still a problem. Apparently it is beyond you alone.

If you had a 100-pound log that had to be moved, and someone offered to help, wouldn't you let them? For many people, in the beginning, a group of others with the same problem can be used as that power greater than yourself that can help restore you to sanity. When you connect with a Clutterers Anonymous group, the first thing you realize is that you are not the only one with the problem; you are not simply crazy. Clutter addiction is a real thing.

By listening to others who have walked the path you are beginning, their methods, how they used the twelve steps to find a better way of living, you will come to see the difference between living in the problem and living in the solution. You will hear stories about people just like you, those who thought their situation was hopeless, that they were doomed to live a cluttered life, only to find hope through the process of incorporating the twelve steps set forth by Alcoholics Anonymous into their lives.

If you are not yet ready to accept a God of your understanding into your life, are unable or unwilling to ask for help through a spiritual connection, there is help through a human connection. That power greater than yourself can be the power of "us," of "we," of not having to stand alone against the addiction. Once you become a part of the "we," from that moment on, you never have to be alone again, and you have a choice each day to live an uncluttered life.

Whether it's through connecting through spirituality or humanity, the power of two is always greater than the power of one.

Sponsors

Although sponsorship was not part of the original twelve-step program, over the years as the world changed, needs changed, and the program has adapted. Some follow the old ways by simply using the people at the meetings to help them through. Others find it helpful to find one person who will help guide them through the program.

If you think you might benefit from having a sponsor, look for someone who has successfully incorporated the twelve steps into their life, a person whose story you can relate to, who will be available to you when you need them. If you are new to the program, and don't yet know people very well, you might ask someone to be your temporary sponsor. That's an acceptable practice. You can see how it works, and if it doesn't work out, you can move on without feeling as if you are stepping on their toes.

Sponsorship is not just about you. It also helps the person who is doing the sponsoring. Don't feel bad about asking someone for help, because giving it away helps keep them from falling back into their addiction. Someone helped them, they will help you, and some day, when you have something to give back, you will help another person. That's how a twelve-step program works.

It is also acceptable to have more than one sponsor. Meet your needs wherever you need to. You may find that working with one person on the steps is helpful, but that you are drawn to another person who has a stronger spiritual program. There is nothing wrong with asking that person to be your spiritual sponsor. If the sponsor you've been working with is truly interested in what's best for you, he or she will not be offended. Your sponsor should always encourage you to follow your heart, to do whatever you need to do that works for you.

Be wary of people who seek control. A sponsor is not a parent, guru, or your boss. You are an adult and should be treated with respect, not talked down to or treated like a child. If you see that happening, a red flag should go up.

If the person you asked to sponsor you has forgotten that he knows some answers, and has come to believe that he is the answer, you need to rethink your choice. A twelve-step program is about choices. The steps are suggested, but we work with them in our own time, in our own way, until we find what works for us. An inflexible sponsor is one who believes there is only one way to work the program: their way.

There are things about your life that you will be willing to reveal in meetings, and some things that you will be more comfortable telling one person. Your sponsor is there to listen, to allow you to talk it through until you come to your own conclusion. Since the sponsor is likely not a priest or physician, there is no guarantee it won't be repeated; therefore it simply falls to a matter of trust. For the clutter addict, most of whom have serious trust issues, that will be a big deal. It's another opportunity to walk through the fear, to make another crack in the clutter wall.

You should be able to tell a sponsor anything without fear of being judged. You should be able to bring them into your home, and your life, no matter how messy it is, and know they understand. If you have a specific problem with a step, in spiritual matters, an effective sponsor will simply share their experience, strength, and hope with you. If they don't have something to share that might help, they will guide you to another member of the meeting who might have some insight for you.

Remember that people are human, and humans are not perfect. Do not put unrealistic expectations on the person you choose as your sponsor. After all, they are not putting expectations on you. A twelve-step program is for one day at a time, but for the rest of your life. We all have good days and bad days.

Your job in the sponsor-addict relationship is to be honest, listen, and be open to looking at things from a different perspective. You have chosen to embark upon a path that your sponsor has already traveled. He or she understands the fear, the pitfalls, the hurdles that must be overcome to achieve daily recovery.

For many who suffer from clutter addiction, a sponsor can make all the difference. Imagine having one person in your life, available to you 24/7, who accepts you totally; one individual who knows everything about you and loves you anyway, who supports you in all your decisions. That person will always be honest with you, because the least we owe someone we care about is the truth. Aren't those the qualities you have been searching for in others all your life? The catch is that anything you expect from another person, you must be willing to give yourself.

If you are considering getting a sponsor, or becoming a sponsor, take it seriously. It's not a tea party once a week. It is a committed relationship that will affect both individuals involved. It is a relationship that must be built on an honest exchange, holding nothing back, with no conditions. Like the twelve-step program, you will get out of this relationship what you are willing to put into it.

Step 3

The Spiritual Experiment

*Made a decision to turn our will and our lives over
to the care of God as we understood God.*

S TEP 3, "Made a decision to turn our will and our
lives over to the care of God as we understood
God," is the big one. This step seems to be one of the
most difficult for many people in early recovery. Even
though Clutterers Anonymous is not a religious program, it is based in spirituality. This can be a stumbling
block for those who believe that if they can't see it,
touch it, or hear it, it doesn't exist, and for those who
have had unpleasant religious experiences.

But, there it is, and we must find a way to deal with it. At this point, your mind may be saying, "If I wanted to pray this clutter away, I'd go to church." What this step is suggesting you do is miles away from what you may have experienced in a religious setting.

One way to deal with Step 3 is to look at it as an experiment. You're surely not averse to experiments. You have probably tried any number of things to overcome the clutter up to this point. If they had worked, you wouldn't need Clutterers Anonymous. It's worth a try. If it doesn't work, you can go back to whatever else it was you were doing.

For the first part of the experiment, listen. Open your mind to what others have done that worked for them. You may have to try several things until you find what is comfortable for you, or at least what you are willing to attempt. You don't have to believe it, or understand it. After all, just because you think something won't work doesn't mean it won't. Your best efforts, and beliefs, brought you to where you are at the moment. Perhaps it's time to consider something different.

There is a reason Step 3 begins with "Made a decision." This is not just something that happens. You need to make a conscious decision to do it. Decisions are funny things. You've probably sat in your nest over and over and made decisions to change your behavior, only to continue living the same way. Imagine walking to the top of a building. Make a decision to walk down. Until you take that first step, you are going nowhere. In a twelve-step program, a decision is a commitment to action.

For those clutter addicts who simply wade through each day, overwhelmed with simple life experiences, so spiritually confused that they are paralyzed, it takes everything they have to survive. Having lived in a survival mode for so long, the thought of turning things over, the idea of surrender to anything can be daunting. It's as if they are holding on to sanity by a thread, and if they let go, if they walk out of the clutter of body, mind, and spirit, it's like being stripped naked for all the world to see. A frightening thought.

First things first. It's time to figure out a God of your understanding. Unlike religions, which tell you what to believe, a twelve-step program allows you to choose what God is. You are in charge of the universe, or at least your corner of it. Remember, it's an experiment. You can imagine your God any way you like. If it helps, picture him, or her, in physical form with all the attributes that you wish God would have. Most human beings spend a great deal of time looking for that one person who will love them unconditionally, allow them to be exactly who they are, who will be totally support-ive and always want the best for them, no matter what their life choices are. If that's what you're looking for, that's what the God of your understanding could be. Your God could live in the sky, on top of a mountain, or you might carry him around with you in your heart everywhere you go. It's entirely up to you.

Once you have a God pictured in your mind, you can begin to work the third step. Because most clutter ad-dicts have a tendency to overwhelm themselves, and see life as one big job that they couldn't possibly take on, it's important to take things down to small bites. Look at one thing in your life you are having a problem with. It could be a financial situation, a personal situation, even a legal matter. Try turning that one thing over, for one day. Do it again the next day, and the next, until it is resolved.

When you turn a problem over to the God of your understanding, you must leave it there. You know you've left it to God when you stop worrying about it and trying to fix it. If you need help with that, try a God box. A God box is a box with a lid that you have written the word *God* on top of. Write your problem on a slip of paper and place it inside the box. Close the lid. If you start worrying, you must take the paper out. When you are ready, put it back in. Do that until you are able to leave it there.

Your experiment is in progress. Understand that the results are out of your hands. Pay attention to what happens. Know that people who have helped you, that letter that came in the mail, an unexpected phone call, even a way to make extra money are not coincidences. The results may be very different than you think they should be, but they will always be for your best in the long run.

Once that situation is resolved, do not let your God box become a part of the clutter wall. Keep it in a very special place, a place where you can see it, where you know it's always there, to remind you to continue using it. As you learn to turn each thing over, one at a time, to this God of your understanding, you will be amazed. You will no longer feel that it is you against the world. When you begin to truly feel a connection—and it gets stronger with use—you will come to understand that you are never alone, and that with God in your corner, all things are possible.

Faith is like a muscle. The more you use it, the stronger it gets. Flex that muscle. It is important to prepare yourself for the steps to come. The first three steps are about opening your mind and nurturing your soul. The steps to come are about putting your faith into action. They help you understand what happened, why it happened, and what you can do to make it better.

One Day at a Time

Although one day at a time is important, for the clutter addict, one "thing" at a time is just as important. Clutter addicts have wide vision. It's as if, if they can't do it all, they do nothing. They justify doing nothing by seeing life as one big ball of clutter that can't possibly be sorted out.

Even when they become inclined to clean things up, they simply move the piles from one location to the next, or clean out something that ends up making a new pile. And, the same attitude carries over into other aspects of their life. Decisions are like the piles of clutter. Letting go of things is a conscious decision. Holding onto things is too.

Why is it so important to hold onto things, many of which we will never use, some we don't even know we have? We tell ourselves we might need it. However, it's not really about the things. It's about holding onto the past, about holding onto old feelings, outdated reasons, and justifications, in case we need them. And, we do need them. They are the anchors that keep us from moving forward and living our lives to the fullest extent. They are the excuse we need not to succeed in life. They are the things that keep us from taking risks in life that will bring us to true happiness and peace.

The piles, the things, are the excuse clutter addicts use not to participate in life. As long as they are over-whelmed with so much to do, even though they never get it done, there is no time for introspection, for deep relationships with others. They are safe behind their wall, focused on all the things.

One day at a time is about stepping out of your com-fort zone. It's saying that just for this one day, I will do something different. You can start with baby steps. Just for today, I will return everything I use to its place. Today, I will make a decision and stick to it. Today, I will make a shopping list and not detour from it. Today, I will go for a walk and smile at people, talk to people, engage in being a part of the world around me. Today, I will ask a God of my understanding to help me.

Each little thing you do differently will make you stronger for the next. It might be scary at first, but as you put yourself out there in one thing, one day at a time, you will begin to see the world opening up to you.

It's like a crack in the wall that the sun can shine through. It can warm you, body, mind, and soul.

In no time, you will be looking into your own eyes in the mirror and recognizing the person you are, what you are capable of, what you want out of life. You will know there is hope. As you become more introspective, there will be an understanding that it is time to let go of things of the past that no longer enhance your life, and worry over a future that you have no control over. You have only this day, this moment, to live your life to the best of your ability.

I'm sure you've seen stories in newspapers and on television about others whose lives have changed in one day. They worked hard, accumulated those things they deemed important, thought they had a secure future, only to have it all wiped out by a flood, a hurricane, a devastating illness. These are the things over which you have no control. However, you do have this day, this moment, and choices of what to do with that gift.

It always fascinates me to hear what people say after a terrible event. They say things like, "At least we're alive. . . . We have our health, our family, friends, and we have the opportunity to rebuild our lives." They are grateful for the most basic things. They are grateful for the moment, the day, the sunshine, enough to eat, and a warm, dry place to sleep. Ah, that we could all be that grateful each day for the most basic of needs being met. Imagine what it would be like not to worry about anything more than that. It's possible when we learn to live to the fullest each day.

The past is just that. It's past. There is no going back to change it, all the regrets won't make it anything more or less than it was, and holding onto it is like being attached to a bungee cord. No matter how we try to move forward, it keeps pulling us back.

The future is about tomorrow, and we never know for sure there will be a tomorrow, or if there is, what it will bring. All the worry in the world, all the hoarding of stuff, all the planning will not secure our place in the future. The future is unknown. If we worry over it, it robs of us the moments that we know belong to us.

This moment, this day, could be the best of your life, could be a life-changing experience, might be the last you have, so you must decide whether to let it slip by unnoticed because you are worried about something that might never happen or something that has already happened. There is an old saying that goes, "If you have one foot in yesterday and one foot in tomorrow, you will fall on your butt today."

When you begin to understand the concept of living in each day, attacking life one thing at a time, letting go of what is of no use to you, not only will your space open up, but your mind will open to a new clarity about what is important and about your place in the world. You are worthy of everything life has to offer when you believe you are and open yourself to it each day. It's like opening your arms wide and saying, "Here I am; do with me what you will, and I will live my life boldly and unafraid this day." You will be amazed at what the world is waiting to share with you.

Step 4

Pen to Paper

*Made a searching and fearless moral
inventory of ourselves.*

S TEP 4, "Made a searching and fearless moral inventory of ourselves," is the beginning of the journey into self-discovery.

The reason we are reluctant to say out loud, "My name is _____, and I am a clutter addict," is that saying it makes it a reality. When we admit that, we feel we have to do something about it. The same is true with writing out an inventory of our lives. When we see it in black and white, the facts become undeniable.

When considering Step 4, remember that half-measures don't give you half-recovery. They give you nothing. It is important to do this step as thoroughly as your memory allows. It's time to be brutally honest. It's not the time to gloss over those situations and feelings that are difficult to look at.

One way to begin an inventory is to make a life line. It's a graph done by years. Go back as far as you can recall, and year by year, show whether it was a high, a low, or a straight line. Now, think about why you drew each year the way you did. It will help you find a starting point for your inventory.

Make three columns: 1. What happened? 2. How did you feel about it then? 3. How do you feel about it now? How you feel about it now will tell you what you need to work on. If you are still holding onto the feelings you originally felt, they are probably still affecting your life.

You will be searching for situations that caused fear, anger, resentments, jealousy, self-pity, dishonesty, and intolerance. It will be tempting to see other people's involvement in the situation, but the inventory is about you. No matter what others did to you, what you'll be looking for is your reaction, the feelings that you are still holding onto, allowing to affect you.

Living in fear keeps us from living life to the fullest. Those risks we are afraid of taking hold us back from some wonderful people and experiences. When you are angry at another person or situation, the anger owns you. The other person isn't the one unable to sleep, pacing the floor holding onto terrible thoughts, unable to focus on their life—that would be you. If we hold onto anger long enough, it becomes a resentment that can fester like a cancer. It may not manifest itself physically, but it certainly has an emotional and psychological effect. The best definition for resentment I ever heard was "anger turned inward."

Jealousy and self-pity go hand in hand. Self-pity is "Why me?" and jealousy is "Why not me?" These are two of the most self-centered emotions, and they feed into other emotions like resentment, anger, and intolerance. The situations of your life were what they were and are what they are. You cannot change the past, but you can change your attitude about the past. The present is within your control. You can choose to sit around feeling sorry for yourself, or you can find something to be grateful for. Those who are happy and content in their own lives do not waste their time comparing themselves to others. They are happy for others who find their way. It's not about jobs, money, possessions, but about how we treat ourselves and others that is important. I believe that, when all is said and done, we are accountable for our relationships with other human beings and ourselves.

Dishonesty is living against yourself. Through all the clutter, the lies, we know the truth. The truth is that we want to be who we really are, a part of things, to know that sense of belonging. Doing a fourth step brings that to the forefront. By taking a hard, brutal look at those behaviors that are incongruent with who we really are, we come to understand that we have been living in conflict with ourselves. People can't live in constant conflict with themselves and expect to be happy and content.

If you are intolerant and critical of others, it is about focus. As long as you can keep your focus on other people, you don't have to look at yourself. It's an ego thing. You may need others to look down on to feel good about yourself. It's like saying, "My life may not be perfect, but it's better than hers." The fourth step brings the focus back to self. You will be looking at your part in all situations. What did you do to make it better, or worse? If you want others to be tolerant of your beliefs and actions, you must give them the same.

You may think the clutter wall is made up of things, bits and pieces of your life, but the wall was built, inch by inch, through emotions—unresolved emotions. In working a fourth step, fearlessly, you become aware of those emotions. Where did it start? When did it begin? Why are you still holding onto it? How is it affecting your life? These and many other questions will be answered through this step.

Remember, it is a moral inventory of your life, your thoughts, feelings, and actions. It's about becoming accountable. You are not to focus on what others said or did, but on how you responded. Were you dishonest, intolerant, filled with jealousy and self-pity, did you react with anger, which later turned into resentment?

The fourth step is the step of self-awareness. As you search through your past, become fearless in your assessment of your part in things, you will begin to see holes in your clutter wall, open spaces where you might walk through, hope that there is a life for you outside the wall.

Easy Does It

You may think it incongruent to say, "Easy does it," to a clutter addict. To those outside, it may appear that they don't do much. That's not true. It is time consuming to maintain the wall of clutter and stay distracted 24/7. Clutter addicts are busy, busy, busy.

Clutter addicts are not lazy, although they feel tired a great deal of the time. Their problem is priorities and lack of focus in their living space. I mention living space because they are usually very different in the workplace. If fact, they tend to go to the other extreme on the job. That goes back to the image thing. They act like super-heroes trying to protect their identities.

A job serves two purposes. It is a distraction on a daily basis and helps us justify being too tired to deal with a home life. Jobs are public, home is personal. And, that personal stuff is what they are trying to hide from behind the clutter.

"Easy does it" is about finding balance, about taking things one at a time, not making mountains out of molehills, about setting reasonable goals and following through. Perhaps it would be better to say, "Easy does it, but do it."

In the beginning, through using the twelve-step program, the best the addict may be able to do is to stop adding to the clutter wall and to begin to recognize the distractions. Once reality sets in and the problem is faced head-on, the healing can begin. The problem has existed for some time. The reason for the problem began even before that. The healing will take time. That's where "Easy does it" comes in. Don't expect miracles overnight.

The most difficult part of working the twelve steps for the clutter addict is taking it easy, not looking at it as something that has to be accomplished all at once. Each step will take however much time it takes for that individual, and will happen when they are ready to do it. It would be easy for the addict to look at the entire program and yell, "I'm overwhelmed!" However, that would just be another excuse. The twelve-step program works when we implementing each step into our lives, one step at a time, one day at a time, sometimes one moment at a time. Easy does it, but do it.

Step 5

Secrets

Admitted to God, to ourselves, and to another human
being the exact nature of our wrongs.

S TEP 5, "Admitted to God, to ourselves, and to another human being the exact nature of our wrongs,"
might seem like an unnecessary step, since you have already written out an inventory of your life in Step 4.
Didn't you already admit to yourself those things that
fed into your addiction? Even so, they are still your
secrets.

You are only as sick as your secrets, so when you consider doing this all-important step, remember what I
said about half-measures. There will not be relief unless

you tell it all. Yes, even those secrets that you were going to take to your grave.

A God of your understanding is always available to you. You can talk to him or her whenever and wherever you want. You might think, Why do I have to say these things out loud to God? Doesn't God already know what I've done? Saying it out loud is much like seeing it in black and white in the fourth step. Once the words are spoken, it becomes more of a reality, and when you accept it as real, you can begin searching for solutions.

One aspect of this that might seem confusing is that you are looking for your part in things. If your problems began in childhood, with molestation, physical, emotional, or psychological abuse, that wasn't your fault. Perhaps others have disappointed you, abandoned you, even left you with the trauma of their death. These are the things you didn't cause, had no control over. What could your part in these things possibly be?

What have you done with whatever trauma happened to you? Have you used the pain from the past as an excuse to self-destruct? Have you used it to hold yourself apart from others, or to justify hurting them? Have you built a wall of clutter that has gotten so big that you are imprisoned? Behind that wall, do you live with anger, resentment, intolerance, self-pity, jealousy, dishonesty, and fear?

If you are an adult, and are still living with pain from the past, there is something to consider. When anything causes you that much pain, and you hold onto it that hard, you are getting something out of it. You must figure out what the payoff is. For many, it is an excuse, or justification, to live a fear-based life and to blame it on other people and past experiences.

It may not seem obvious that you are living in fear. However, clutter addiction, like all other addictions, is based in fear. It is your buffer between you and the world, and other people. It is the excuse you use not to make commitments, to keep you from intimate relationships, and from reaching your full potential in life. It keeps you from the true happiness that we all deserve in this life.

Step 5 is not about saying, "Look what they did to me," but about asking yourself, "What have I done with what was done to me?" One way to look at it is that whoever "they" were, whatever "they" did, if you are still letting it affect your life today, they win.

Another way to help resolve the past is to understand that people don't wake up one day and decide who to be. Just like you, other people are the result of their life experiences. They are the way they are because of what happened to them. Perhaps they've made the decision to hold onto their secrets even if doing so destroys their relationships and their lives. You have a choice not to do that, and Step 5 will help you.

Secrets only have power as long as they are kept secret. They live within you, and the fear lives within you that some day, some way, your secrets might see the light of day. What would other people think of you then? You might be surprised. Rather than seeing you as bad, shameful, and disgusting, they might see you as courageous, strong, and admirable for facing your problems head-on and finding a way out. Everyone has secrets, has had problems in their lives, and most people think theirs are the worst because it happened to them. You are no different. Others might not think your secrets are all that bad.

When you begin the search for another human being to do your fifth step with, there are several things to consider. If you are attending meetings, watch and listen. As you get to know others who have the same problem as you, pay attention to who makes sense, who is leading the life they are talking about. Are they happy, at peace? Do they walk their talk? That's important, because it is too easy to tell others how to do something even though we can't do it ourselves.

If you are concerned about your anonymity, try not to pick a person who has a habit of discussing other members outside the meetings. To be able to confide completely, you must be able to trust that your secrets are safe.

Another clutter addict is usually a good choice. He or she can relate to your problem. Having lived through what you are in the middle of, another addict won't be as prone to judge. However, the person you choose doesn't have to be a member of a twelve-step program. You might feel more comfortable with a member of the clergy, a trusted friend, even a relative with whom you can confide.

Once you've made the choice, pick a time and place with no distractions to meet with that person. It is important to turn off the phones, not have children and pets around, and leave the music for another time. Stay out of public places, because this can be a very emotional time.

If you have trouble getting started, you might allow the other person to read your written fourth step. Then, discuss it. Another way is simply to begin at the beginning and tell your story, revealing your secrets as you go. You are not there to talk about the wrongs of others, but about the exact nature of *your* wrongs. You are not there to make yourself look good by minimizing your actions. You are not there to play the martyr, make excuses, or justify your actions. It is the moment of truth. It is an opportunity to get it all out. This is not the time to hold back. It is the time to be brutally honest.

When you're done, you will be amazed that the world didn't come to an end just because your secrets are out there. You are still there, the other person is still there, and the only thing that happened is you have taken your power back. Once a secret is spoken out loud, it never has the power to hurt you again. Many people feel as if a weight has been lifted from their shoulders. It is a real burden to carry those heavy secrets around for all those years, protecting them behind that wall of clutter.

Only when you have successfully completed your fifth step will you understand that you no longer need to protect yourself, your secrets, from the world. When that happens, the healing that began in the first four steps will be put into action. If there is nothing left to protect, there is no need for the physical or emotional walls. It is time to begin pulling the walls down.

Only by the Grace of God, Go I

When I think of "Only by the grace of God, go I," I'm reminded of a story that was shared with me years ago.

Many twelve-step groups have conferences, round-ups, and campouts for their members. The young man who told me this story was attending his first campout. His had been a life filled with abuse, tragedy, and later, addictions. However, things were turning around with the help of the twelve-step program. He was full of gratitude, but at the same time, he suffered from a great deal of pride in having overcome his addictions.

Late at night, when the campfire was lit, all would gather around the blaze and share their stories and their gratitude for their new lives. The young man settled in between an elderly man and a woman who looked to be in her early thirties. As they said the prayer, read the steps and traditions, his mind was working furiously on what he would say when it was his turn. He just knew his was the worst story ever. He would blow their minds.

He could barely hear the other stories because he was so excited to share. His turn was moving closer. His anxiety grew. The woman was next, then him. He could barely contain himself.

The woman, we'll call Anne, said, "I am so grateful to be here tonight among all of you." She shared about the past, what first brought her to a twelve-step program, and the wonderful five years she'd had since. Then, Anne said, "Two weeks ago I was diagnosed with inoperable cancer."

That got the young man's attention. He looked at the attractive young woman, her blond hair curling around a pixie face. He must have misheard.

"I have around six months, or less," Anne continued. A tear escaped. She wiped it away and forced a smile. "I am so grateful for my husband. He is the kindest, most caring man ever, and he will be here to raise my girls. I am so grateful for this program that has given me five good years with my family, my husband, my kids."

Tears welled in the young man's eyes. This woman was dying. . . . In six months, she would no longer be there. It wasn't fair.

The last thing she said was, "If I were given the choice to live out the rest of my life the way I was, or to have five good years the way it has been, I wouldn't even have to think about it. So, I want to thank all of you for helping me. I am so grateful."

It was finally the young man's turn. He passed.

We all think our pain is the worst, because we are the one suffering from it. Pain is relative. Just because one person has had several divorces, and doesn't think it's any big deal, doesn't mean another person, who had a long-term marriage, who was truly in love, shouldn't be suffering. We all have to walk through our own pain the best way we can. A twelve-step program helps us to understand that.

Only by the grace of God, go I, is not about comparing our pain to anyone else's, but about knowing that all we are, the opportunity we've been given for a better way of life, is through grace. The twelve-step program is not a punishment, but a gift that is truly inspired.

"Where there is gratitude, there is no attitude." "If I can't have what I want, let me want what I have." "I am exactly where I'm supposed to be today." "God doesn't pull a drowning person from the water just to throw him back in." These are some of the sayings that one might hear when the topic is gratitude or the grace of God.

It's been said that if a person thanks the God of their understanding for three things each day, it will help them stay out of self-pity, jealousy, and depression. It's worth a try. What does it take, a few minutes of your life every day? And, what if it works?

For the clutter addict, "If I can't have what I want, let me want what I have" is of special significance. As their life changes in a twelve-step program, so will their surroundings. It's time to figure out exactly what you have. Did you find that special item, the one you thought you couldn't live without six months ago, under the bed with the price tag still attached? Apparently, you didn't need it. Let it go. More important, figure out exactly what you have, what you need, what you can let go of, and do it. You can't know what you need until you know what you have.

While sorting, as you pick each thing up to decide what to do with it, do it with a grateful attitude. You can be grateful you have it, or that you can give it to someone else who needs it more. Begin to understand the value of each item you have. Tell yourself what it would be like to not have it, to be unable to afford it. When you begin to see the value of all items, whether to keep them or give them away, they will become real treasures.

When you treasure something, you will take care of it, find a very special place for it, be grateful for it. It's better to have a few things that are meaningful than a roomful of stuff that means nothing.

Imagine there was a disaster. What would you want to save? What would you reach for first? Would it be enough that your life was saved, the lives of your family and pets? Disasters, like health issues, can put things in perspective in a hurry.

When we learn the value of things, the value of life, the value of health, so many things that we should be grateful for, it teaches us about compassion and tolerance of others. We will no longer be able to look away from the homeless man sitting on a curb with a sign asking for help or work. We come to understand that under other circumstances that could be us. Would we want others to look through us as if we didn't exist, to walk around us as if we were diseased, to ignore our cry for help?

Through working the steps, we will know that as much as we are where we are for a reason today, other people are where they are for a reason. We are not on a need-to-know basis. That's between them and the God of their understanding. However, when we encounter a person in distress, we have been given an opportunity to make a choice. And, when we make that choice, we must say to ourselves, "Only by the grace of God, go I."

It's not simply about helping others in a twelve-step program. It's about joining the human race, getting involved in humanity. It's about making that commitment each day to treat others the way you would wish to be treated. We have all been blessed with certain gifts, but it is what we do with those gifts that makes a difference in the world.

The next time you are walking down the street, and you encounter someone with a disability, a person who looks different, someone in dire straits, a person crying out for help, remember, that could be you, and it's only by the grace of God that it isn't. Act accordingly.

By living with an attitude of gratitude, no matter your situation in life, and understanding the true value of things, you will finally know what it is to have enough. Whatever you have at that moment, as long as you are living the God of your understanding's will, is enough.

Changes

Were entirely ready to have God remove
all these defects of character.

Humbly asked God to remove our shortcomings.

S TEP 6, "Were entirely ready to have God remove
all these defects of character," and Step 7, "Humbly
asked God to remove our shortcomings," are about
willingness and change.

If you have successfully worked your way through
the first five steps to the best of your ability, two things
should have taken place. You will have found a God of

your understanding and an awareness of those things that keep you from peace and happiness.

Awareness is important, because you can't become willing to do something about your defects of character until you can put names to them. What is a character defect? It's anything you do that keeps you from the life the God of your understanding wants for you.

You may not yet know what God wants for you, but it should be easy enough to figure out what God *doesn't* want for you. Faith is about a lack of fear. When you live a fear-based life, filled with resentments and frustration, overwhelmed on a daily basis, hidden behind a wall of clutter, unable to give yourself fully to anything or anyone, you can be of no real value to yourself. When you don't value yourself as a product of something so wondrous, you will be of little value to others.

Questions arise when considering character defects. They are like old friends we are not sure we want to let go. We know what to expect. We are comfortable with it. It has been a part of our life for so long, it's like a pain we've gotten so used to. It would be missed if it disappeared. For a person who has held onto anger and resentments for years, feeling love and compassion may be like trying on a coat that doesn't fit. We may not be sure what to do with it.

Deep within ourselves, we know that when we release our character defects, our bridges will be burned. There will be no going back. There will be no excuses left when we want to be self-destructive. It's a big commitment.

Rationalization and justifications are your enemies when working Steps 6 and 7. Step 6 says, "Were *entirely* ready to have God remove *all* these defects of character." It's not about thinking we can pick and choose, tell ourselves this defect isn't really that bad, maybe it's just a character trait. We have a right to resent this person or that. For God's sake, look what they did. It's healthy to hold onto some fear. We don't want to set ourselves up to get hurt again. We deserve to be angry when someone wrongs us. When thoughts such as these go through our minds, we are not entirely ready.

Entirely ready means just that. It is total surrender of self to the God of our understanding. We can begin by praying for the willingness to let go of our character defects. That's our job in this step . . . to become willing. We cannot remove our defects, or we would have already done that. The step says the God of our understanding will remove them when we are ready.

More questions arise. What will I be like without my character defects? Will I have to be good all the time?

Do I want to be that good? Are these changes some-thing I can deal with? That's the kicker . . . change. Change is not comfortable for most human beings, but addicts have a particular problem with change. Clutter addicts, like most other addicts, have become accustomed to a certain way of life. It may not be the greatest, but it's what we are used to. The fear of change will be a leap of faith.

What will you be like? Through the steps, with help from a God of your understanding, you will become the person you really are. It won't be necessary to put on that "I'm fine" face in public and return in private to your cluttered life. You will discover that you have a choice to trust others, to be involved in life. You will come to understand that with a God of your understanding in your corner, there are no limitations.

Will you have to be good all the time? Living in the truth of who you are is all you have to do. When you believe you are a product of God, you will live that way. It happens through faith. You are not perfect, and you will never be in this lifetime, so all you have to do is the best you can for yourself, and for others, each day. It's okay to be human, because you are human.

When you have become willing, it's time to say the words. Step 7 is asking the God of your understanding to remove all the things that keep you from the best life you can have. You will be amazed. Situations arise, and you find yourself seeing them from a new perspective, from a place of love, compassion, and understanding. You will come to understand that just as much as you are where you are at this moment for a reason, other people are where they are for a reason. There will be a knowing deep inside that each life has a purpose, and you need to stay in yours and allow others theirs.

One by one, the burdens of the cluttered life will be lifted from you until you know the lightness of peace and happiness. Life will not be coincidental. Everything that happens, every person you meet, will have meaning. Even those things that are difficult to live through will be for your best in the long run, because there is a lesson to be learned from every experience.

Once the walls are no longer needed, they will come down.

Live and Let Live

The wall of clutter is the outward manifestation of the wall clutter addicts build around themselves for protection. What is it they need to protect themselves from? It is fear of getting hurt. Like a wounded animal that seeks a small, dark place to feel safe and lick their wounds, clutter addicts hide behind the wall.

All addictions are self-centered. It's as if they are saying to the world, "My problems are greater than yours, so I have the right to do this to myself and others." That is the justification for holding themselves apart from the world and other people. Many clutter addicts refuse to watch anything but shopping shows and house design shows on television because news shows bring the world into their space. Others watch the news constantly, dwelling on the evils of the world, and of other people, to rationalize living in fear.

It is a big world full of unique people. Relationships are complex because of our differences. They can also be fascinating. The greatest joys and biggest frustrations in life involve other people. So, what happens with clutter addicts who have made the decision to live in fear and remove themselves from the greater population? They miss out . . . not only on their own lives, but in fully sharing in the lives of others.

Live and let live is about changing perspectives. The beginning of changing one's perspective is to look at commonality instead of differences. All human beings have things in common. We all have basic needs: food, water, clothes, shelter, to love and be loved, to be treated with decency and dignity, and to feel safe in an unsure world.

Just like you, other people don't wake up one day and decide who to be. We are all products of our own experiences in life. And even though our experiences may differ, our feelings are similar. When someone we care for dies, we feel sadness. If someone wrongs us, we are disappointed, frustrated, even angry. A birth can bring us great joy. Another's kindness makes us feel great appreciation. We all feel a myriad of emotions throughout our lives.

The emotions we feel aren't as important as what we do with them. Addicts, no matter what their addiction, have decided they need a buffer between themselves and their emotions. To accomplish that end, they must also keep the buffer, or addiction, between themselves and other people. For clutter addicts, it's the stuff . . . piles and piles of stuff that has taken on great importance, the never-ending job of cleaning up, moving things around, that keeps them from feelings. As long as they stay overwhelmed, keep themselves distracted, there isn't room for anything else.

Behind the wall, the clutter addict's world becomes smaller and smaller. To justify the way they live, they blame others. Intolerance rears its ugly head. Everyone who enters their life is under intense scrutiny. To stay in the clutter addict's life, the other person must continually prove his or her loyalty. Clutter addicts will tell themselves they are the way they are for numerous reasons. For instance, "People are never what they seem to be. They say one thing and do another. How am I supposed to deal with that? Just when I think I know what to expect, the relationship changes. Don't they have any morals and values? What were they thinking when they did what they did? It's so clear to me. Why can't they see it? Why do I bother? What is the point? When I don't agree with what they are doing, it would be hypocritical of me to be around them."

The truth is that people do the best they can with what they have to work with at the moment. When I was fifteen years old, I became a parent. It wasn't that I didn't want to be a good parent; I didn't know how. I was ignorant about what to do. I was a child raising a child without a clue. I did the best I could with what I had to work with at that time in my life. That was true for me and is true for others.

Other people held unrealistic expectations of me, saying that if I was old enough to have a child, I should know how to raise him. It was an attitude of "You made your bed, lie in it." Because of others' expectations, I thought I should know how to take care of a child, but I didn't. Obviously, there was something wrong with me. I made a mistake; I not only paid dearly for it, so did an innocent child.

Expectations are dangerous, not only for the person who has the expectations cast upon her, but for the person holding the expectations. When we expect others to do what we think they should, when, and how, we inevitably end up disappointed, frustrated, or angry. If the person wants to stay in our life, in whatever relationship, and they can't live up to our expectations of them, it feeds into poor self-esteem, guilt, and shame.

If you want to put expectations on another person, try this: "I expect you to live your life to the best of your ability, to do whatever it is that will make you happy and content, and I wish you well in all things. I love you because of who you are, not because of what you do, or don't do. I don't have to agree with everything you do, but I would fight for your right to do it."

Because of the small world clutter addicts live in, the self-centeredness of addiction, they tend to believe other people's actions are about them. They are not. People spend their lives attempting to fulfill their own needs, whatever they might be at the time. People aren't doing things to them; they are doing things "for" themselves.

To be able to live and let live, that is the first thing that must be understood.

If we want to have healthy relationships with other people, first we must have a healthy relationship with ourself. That means we focus on our own life. We stop blaming others for our feelings and how we deal with them. We take total responsibility for our actions. Only then will we come to understand that to live and let live means exactly that. We stay in our business, and we leave others to theirs. We are all part of the whole, struggling on a daily basis to get though this life the best way we can.

We don't have to agree with what others think, or do. We don't have to understand it, even condone it, and we can still care for them. We have a choice of who is allowed into our intimate relationships. If someone we love is self-destructive, or destructive to us, we may feel we can't have that person in our life. However, that doesn't mean we have to stop loving them.

Live and let live is about making our own choices, living true to ourselves, and allowing others the same privilege. It's about not putting expectations on others. It's about unconditional love. Isn't that what we all desire—to be loved for who we are, totally and completely, with no conditions? We can have that when we are willing to give it.

The "A" List

Made a list of all persons we had harmed, and became
willing to make amends to them all.

Made direct amends to such people wherever
possible, except when to do so would injure
them or others.

STEP 8, "Made a list of all persons we had harmed, and became willing to make amends to them all," and Step 9, "Made direct amends to such people wherever possible, except when to do so would injure them or others," are an essential part of the recovery process. Through these action steps, we are able to put the past to rest.

When thinking about addicts hurting others, it is easy to imagine an out-of-control drunk or drug addict going on a rampage, being physically and emotionally abusive of those around them. The addict might steal to support their habit, cheat others, lie, commit horrendous acts.

What about clutter addicts? They are not out there doing awful things to hurt people. However, they do cause pain, not only to others, but to themselves. In fact, they should probably place their name at the top of the amends list—considering how they have forced themselves to live the clutter of mind, body, and spirit, carrying the burdens of the past, keeping up a facade, never allowing themselves to get close to anyone.

Can you make amends to yourself? You certainly can, and should. If it helps, look in the mirror and say the words, just as you would to another person. It might seem strange, but it's worth a try. And, as with making amends to another person, there is no room for rationalization or justification. It is about how you have wronged yourself, and how much you regret it.

When you consider the remainder of the list, it can be helpful to pull out that fourth step you worked so diligently on. Were there people you blamed for your circumstances? Did you retaliate in any way? If it was a family member, or close friend, did you withhold your affection? With others, did you gossip, demean them, tell stories that always made you look like the victim? When you got in financial straits, did you lie to someone to get money out of them? At work, did you use underhanded methods to achieve your goals, perhaps cheating someone else out of a position they deserved? All the while, did you run around with a self-righteous attitude, looking down your nose at others, treating them as if they weren't good enough? These are but a few things you might look at when considering whom you owe amends to.

One way to make a list would be:

Person	What I Did	Effect
Myself	Alienated friends and family	Loneliness
	Placed blame on others	Anger, resentments
	Lied	Shame
	Gossiped	Jealousy
	Judged another	Intolerance
	Put up walls	Fear

Person	What I Did	Effect
Parents	Blamed them	Anger, resentments
	Withheld affection	Loneliness
	Treated them badly	Shame, guilt
Friends	Suspicious of their motives and actions	Loneliness
	Judged them harshly	Intolerance
	Blamed them for my feelings	Anger, resentments
	Hid behind my wall	Self-pity

You get the idea. There will be many people on your list, specific people and circumstances, but the effect they have had on your life will be the same. Until these things are resolved, your life may be filled with loneliness, anger, resentments, intolerance, dishonesty, jealousy, shame, and guilt, emotions that are based in fear.

What is it clutter addicts fear? They fear that they will never have enough. However, all the things in the world will never be enough to rid them of their fear. The problem is that the "enough" they are searching for is love. To fulfill that need, it is necessary to open themselves to other people and to the truth of who they are.

If the original fear of life began with situations they believe were brought on by other people, if they were disappointed, hurt, or felt abused, it could have been the beginning of a pattern of placing blame on others. Anger held onto becomes resentment. Resentments cause self-pity. Self-pity feeds jealousy and intolerance. Jealousy and intolerance bring with them dishonesty and malice. Put some or all of these emotions together, and the walls go up.

It stands to reason that if unresolved emotions built the walls, resolving them will help pull them down once and for all. It's time to take a hard look at the reality of the people and situations on your list. Since you are no longer a child, it is important to use an adult point of view.

Imagine that your mother is one of the people on the list. Since she was always overly critical of you, you may blame her for your self-esteem issues, relationship issues with other women, being unable to accept even constructive criticism. However, did you ever think about why she was the way she was? What were her parents like? How did she grow up? Perhaps they had great expectations for her, expectations she didn't fulfill. Maybe she felt like a failure. She may have made the choice to marry and have a family instead of following her dreams. Does she feel cheated? Do you really know her? Have you ever taken the time, or made the effort, to find out how she feels, what her dreams were?

How did you react to the way she treated you? Did you enjoy pushing her buttons? As you got older, did you do things, and say things, that were hateful and cruel? Did you let her know you blamed her for the mess your life was in, the poor choices you've made, the person you are? Have you pushed her out of your life?

The key to Step 8 is first to see the others involved in your life from a different perspective. That will bring you to the understanding that the situations and the people in their lives brought them to their problems and actions. Perhaps they've never had an opportunity to get into a step program, or therapy, to find a way out. Like you, for whatever reason, their lives are out of control.

No matter what they did to you, it's time to consider how you reacted. What, specifically, did you do to them? Have you punished them in various ways, used verbal abuse, withheld affection, or exacted revenge? Be brutally honest, because it is for your benefit. Have you held onto your mother's criticism as an excuse not to live a fulfilled life? After a point, is that her fault? You are an adult and have choices every day. If you've chosen to hold onto that pain, there is a reason. Perhaps it's easier to blame her than to accept responsibility for your choices.

The willingness to make amends for your actions, thoughtless words, your feelings, will come through understanding, compassion, and forgiveness. You can forgive someone without bringing them back into your life. It's about taking care of the unfinished business of the past so that you can get on with your life in a better way. It's about being able to look in the mirror with no regrets. It's about putting closure on situations from the past that have lived in your mind, haunted your dreams, helped build the walls that imprison you.

Even after taking a new look at old situations, and the people involved, if you are still having trouble with willingness, try praying for it.

I remember a woman who, while working her eighth and ninth steps, ran into a problem. She'd worked honestly at making her list. She'd found the willingness, knew forgiveness for everyone on the list, with one exception. It was her stepfather, who had been the bane of her existence. He had been rigid and cruel, critical to the extreme. Her mother committed suicide while married to him.

Many years had passed, but her resentment of him lived on. Finally, when nothing else worked, she prayed about it. Her stepfather lived across the country from her, but if he'd lived in the next town over, she knew she wouldn't be able to approach him, forgive him, or make amends to him. Yes, she'd done everything she could, after her mother's death, to make his life a living hell. However, she believed he deserved everything she could dish out, and more. She kept praying.

The phone rang. It was a nephew of the stepfather. He and the stepfather were in the woman's town for a funeral. The stepfather wanted to see her. The immediate reaction was to decline, but a thought hit her. What if this was the one chance she would have to take care of things? What if this was the answer to her prayers?

They met. As always, he'd been drinking. He was unable to look her in the eyes. Amazingly, she looked at this once formidable man, who now seemed old, small, and pathetic, and knew it was time. She made her amends that day. The only reaction he had was to try to rationalize and justify the person he'd been, and apparently still was. However, she knew it wasn't about him. It was about her. It was about cleaning her own side of the street. She walked away that day, free of the last vestiges of anger and resentment that had lived in her for so many years.

That woman was me. Although I have never had a relationship with my stepfather from that day to this, I no longer hold any ill feelings for him, nor do I wish anything bad upon him. In fact, my hope is that one day he will be given the same opportunity I was given. I have no doubt that day was a gift from the God of my understanding.

Which brings us to Step 9, making the amends. There will be those people you wronged who did absolutely nothing to you except get in your way as you plowed through life, negative emotions in tow. Others have hurt you, so you retaliated. There could be financial issues, work issues, even personal or sexual issues that need to be put to rest.

Some people on your list may have moved away or died. There will be those who dislike you and want nothing more to do with you. Then, there are those whom you've been closest to: relatives, lovers, spouses, ex-spouses, and intimate friends. Where, and how, to begin?

There are two schools of thought on this. Obviously, some amends will be easier to make than others. Some people believe you begin with the easier ones, and work your way up, gathering strength as you go. Others would say to get the hardest ones out of the way first. I don't think it makes any difference. For me, it is those things that bother you most, that go to bed with you at night, haunting your mind and dreams, that slip into your mind during your day, that should be taken care of as quickly as possible.

It doesn't matter if it was a big thing or a small thing, but how it's affecting you. For instance, did you get yourself in a financial bind and lie to someone to get money? Is the guilt and shame alive in your mind daily? Do you get knots in your belly when you run into that person? It needs to be taken care of for your own sake, for your peace of mind.

There are things to consider when you are ready to make amends. Above all, remember, this is about you. You are not there to talk about what the other person did, place blame, or try to justify what you did. You are there to admit you wronged them in some way, and you regret it.

Do not assume, beforehand, that you know how they will react to an amends. If you assume you know something you can't possibly know, it's a good way to talk yourself out of doing what needs to be done. To get optimal results, you need to put aside all thoughts of what they did to you, what kind of person you believe them to be, and any expectations of how they will react.

With those who have passed on, try writing a letter of amends and burning it, or visit the graveside if possible and talk to them. It can be difficult to make amends to those people who have moved away. If you don't know where they are, it may take some investigation on your part. If you locate them, you can call or write a letter. If you can't find them, it may have to be enough that you are willing, and that you pray about it.

If the person is alive, and available to you, find a convenient time for both of you, a quiet place to talk without distractions, and simply tell them you are trying to make changes in your life, what you did to wrong them, and how much you regret it. It may involve finances. Even if you don't have the money at the time, don't put it off. They may be willing to accept a payment plan that you can handle.

There may be legal issues to deal with. If you are willing to make amends to "all" persons you have harmed, that's exactly what it means. It could involve businesses, organizations, even those in the legal system. You are sweeping your side of the street completely clean, so don't shrink from what needs to be done to accomplish it.

For instance, you may have ordered something from the shopping network. By mistake they sent you two and didn't charge you for the second one. If you chose to keep it, every time you look at it you will know you cheated them. To make amends, you could either return it or let them know what happened and pay for it. You aren't doing it for them. You are doing it for you.

In a weak moment, you may have pledged money to an organization, then decided you really didn't want to send it. You made that commitment and need to live up to it. In legal matters, it is no longer acceptable to lie about what happened, to avoid paying those tickets, to walk away from your responsibilities. The relief you get will be in direct accordance with how honest you are.

Now that you know who you need to make amends to, how it should be done, there is something else you need to think about. It's the exception in the last half of the ninth step. In purging your conscience, cleaning your side of the street, you have no right to bring anyone else into it who might get hurt by what you're doing. If you want to admit an affair to your wife or husband, that's fine. However, the other person involved hasn't made that choice and should be left out of it. If you went shopping with a friend, and you both shoplifted merchandise, it's fine for you to make amends both verbally and financially with the store, but any mention of the other person is unacceptable. Each person must come to this step in their life when the time is right for them. The only way you might involve another is with their permission, and not many will be inclined to give it.

Although it's not true in all cases, most people will be open to an honest apology, to a heartfelt amends. It may even inspire some to talk about their part in the situation, possibly to make amends to you. Of course, they are entitled to whatever response they give. The important thing is that we take care of our business.

Every amends you make, every difficult situation you overcome, removes another chunk of the emotional wall that has built the physical walls around you, until you know a new freedom, a new happiness, like that of a child experiencing the world for the first time. You will come to know what it is to trust yourself and others, to put yourself back into a world with no walls, no limitations. Steps 8 and 9, worked thoroughly, will put the past to rest.

Think, Think, Think

I recall the first time I saw "Think, Think, Think" on a sign. What in the world? All I did was think. There seemed to be a continual meeting going on in my head.

I often thought if I could just shut my mind down, life would be a lot easier.

That's not what "Think, Think, Think" is about. It's about learning to act instead of react. When we are in the throes of addiction, we are filled with unexpressed, barely suppressed emotions. And, we never know what will trigger them and break the thin thread of control that holds them in place. Therefore, we may react irrationally to an otherwise rational situation.

How we react is dependent on those unresolved past issues. Holding onto anger and resentment because you grew up with an overly dominant parent might be the reason you react violently to authority figures. Pain over the loss of a loved one can lead to a panic reaction if we begin to get too close to another human being. Betrayals of the past that were never resolved may bring on feelings of mistrust, the reaction being brutal verbal confrontation because of some small infraction others can't understand.

The clutter addict who has not learned yet how to act instead of react might wonder why they don't feel like they have any close friends, why others act funny around them. It may be because of the addict's unusual reactions to otherwise normal situations.

Close friends believe they should be able to think aloud with you. When they begin to feel as if they are walking on eggshells all the time, because of your inappropriate reactions, they will begin to move away. They will say things like, "What was that about? What did I do . . . say? I don't get it."

Working a twelve-step program can teach you how to step back from a situation, think about it sensibly, then make a rational decision of how to act on it. There will be three things to think about: (1) How am I feeling, and why? (2) What did the other person's actions, words, have to do with me? (3) What will be the consequences of my action? Thus, "Think, Think, Think."

The ninth step is particularly helpful because it teaches us to look at others with a new pair of eyes, at situations from another's point of view. When the past is resolved, and we approach situations from a place of understanding, compassion, and love rather than suspicion, frustration, and anger, the results will always be better.

The results I speak of are how you are left feeling at the end of the day. In a twelve-step program, life is about every day, every moment, every situation, person, or event that is put in your path. Each thing has its own importance, and what you do with it determines your character as a human being. You only get this day to live out as best you can, so it counts.

In fact, all the steps, even though you might not understand it at the time, are the tools required for a new and better way of life. Lived out the way they are set up, incorporated into your life on a daily basis, your way of thinking, acting, will change. You will look around you and know that you no longer have to live the way you have; you will come out from hiding behind the walls and discover there is a whole world of new and exciting people and adventures waiting for you. Give it some thought.

Step 10

A Daily Reprieve

*Continued to take personal inventory and when
we were wrong, promptly admitted it.*

STEP 10, "Continued to take personal inventory
and when we were wrong, promptly admitted it,"
reminds us that it's not over. Clutter addiction, like all
other addictions, will not be cured. However, by working the steps, maintaining our spirituality, and staying
with a daily program, we will know recovery.

A program consists of those things you do on a daily
basis that work for you. While you are working the
steps, pay attention to what happens. When you find

something that works for you today, it will probably work tomorrow. As you incorporate these things into your life, they become your program.

People are different, so programs are different. As you attend meetings, and listen to others and how they work their programs, you will try different things until you discover *your* program. For instance, prayer is a very personal thing. Some people feel it necessary to get up early, get down on their knees, and turn their will over to a God of their understanding. It doesn't matter what time you get up, whether you are on your knees, or the words you use. What is important is that you find a time, a place, and a way that works for you each day, and keep doing it.

Right now, you may be thinking that you've worked nine steps, you've found a God of your understanding, and your clutter is gone, so what is the point of continuing meetings, hanging out with other clutter addicts, and feeling like you have to think about this stuff every day?

Imagine that you have a physical illness. You see the doctor. He tells you that you need surgery to correct the problem. You agree. Then, he informs you that after the surgery, to live a happy, healthy, normal life, you will be required to take a pill every day for the rest of your life. You say you can do that. It's worth the effort. It becomes terribly important every day to remember that pill that enables you to have the life you want to live.

In a twelve-step program, the first nine steps are like the surgery, and the last three are the pill. Step 10 is the early phase of maintaining what you found in Clutterers Anonymous that helped you. Was it the understanding and support of other clutter addicts? Was it finding a God of your understanding? How about finding a way to let go of the past, all those unresolved emotions? Has the clutter disappeared, not only from your living space, but from your mind? Are you feeling happy, healthy, and ready to take on the world? Fantastic! Now, do you want to hold onto that feeling?

Addiction is cunning, baffling, powerful, and very patient. It's like that old, comfortable pair of slippers you've put away in the closet. You know the ones. You wore them while you were nesting, when you were sick, in your hiding-out-from-the-world periods. They may be filthy dirty, worn out, terrible looking, but they represent that comfort zone where you lived for so long. And, they are still there waiting, in case you ever want to slip them back on.

For an addict, the addiction is like the slippers, waiting for you to slide back into that old way of thinking, feeling, and acting. Working Step 10 is the answer. It will keep you from ever going back.

At the end of your day, before you sleep, take a personal inventory. What did you give to the day, to others, to yourself? Did you speak sharply to someone because things didn't go as you desired at work? Did you allow someone else to take the blame for something you did? Did you lie about something to your boss, your spouse, a friend? Did you go shopping and spend money allocated for a bill on something frivolous? Did you forget to pray, eat properly, get the rest you needed to take you through the day?

Go back to Steps 8 and 9, and consider whom you may have offended and what your part in it was, without rationalizing or attempting to justify it. If you have wronged someone, it is important to make amends as quickly as possible. It's important because if you don't, it will live in your mind, and become the clutter of the mind that caused the clutter in your world. Remember, it is easier to stay uncluttered than it is to get uncluttered. Each unresolved situation equates to an unresolved emotion, and you know where that leads.

Without using Step 10, it is amazing how quickly you can revert to that person you so desperately wanted to get away from being. When these daily things happen, they may not seem that big at the time. Like your clutter, it wasn't that big when it started. It began with one feeling, putting one thing off, dropping that one piece of paper and not reaching to pick it up. One day, you looked around, and it was overwhelming. It can happen again if you are not willing to take that daily pill, beginning with Step 10.

This step reminds you each day of who you are, what your addiction is, and what you need to be doing for that daily reprieve. There are two things to watch out for: fear and becoming cocky. Faith and fear can't live in the same house, so if you have developed a faith in a God of your understanding, and are working a daily program, there is nothing left to fear. There will be a knowing deep within that if you simply do the next right thing, life will be better. Everything will be okay if you're taking care of business.

Becoming cocky is about looking around one day and seeing how much better your life is: the house is clean, the bills are paid, you have friends and family, you are thriving at work. All is well, and you decide *you* did it. You may have put in the time and the footwork, but you had a lot of help. When you come to believe it was all about you, it becomes easy to forget that God of your understanding who did for you what you could not do for yourself. What about the other people who loved and supported you through the rough times, the hard days when you were ready to give up? What about the steps?

What happens when you get cocky is that you forget. When you forget, there is danger that you will repeat. To keep from getting cocky, never forget what it was like, why you sought help in the first place. If you could have done it on your own, you would have. It's essential to take responsibility for your part in things, good or bad, but it is just as important to give credit where credit is due. In and of yourself, you were unable to accomplish the life you are living.

The danger of forgetting is that you can become lazy in your program, forget to do that morning prayer, your meditation, doing a daily inventory, taking care of things when they come up. And, it can all slip away so quickly. If you take things for granted, like God, the steps, your new life, you could lose them.

Step 10 will enable you to remember. When you remember, how can there be anything but gratitude in your heart? You have been given a second chance in life to live it a better way. You have become a healthier, happier individual who treats yourself, and others, with understanding, compassion, and love. Don't forget to take care of what you have worked so hard for, the gifts that you were given so freely through God and others, and they will be yours for the rest of your days. Always remember, it's only a daily reprieve.

Ego

Ego stands for "edge God out." Steps 2 and 3 introduce us to a God of our understanding that we can turn our will and life over to every day. The point is that it has to be done on a daily basis.

As we work the twelve-step program, life gets better, even if our circumstances don't change. We might not have a better job, more money and things, but we learn to be grateful for what we do have, and we begin to see the possibilities of what the world has to offer, what we are capable of.

With each step we work, we move closer to peace and happiness. Little by little, the clutter wall disappears, and as it goes down, the walls we have built to protect ourselves do the same. We find ourselves back out in the world, living a real life filled with new and exciting experiences and people. Life is good.

What happens when things start going well, when we begin to feel some self-esteem, self-respect, pride in what we have accomplished? Sometimes we forget that we didn't do it alone. The ego can take over, and we believe this is all about us. When that happens, we edge God out.

We allow the ego to take over when we forget what it was like, and what happened to get us out of our mess. That's why it is so terribly important to use our experience, strength, and hope to help others who are at the beginning of the same journey. This serves two purposes. It helps us stay conscious of where we've been, where we are, and how we got there. When we stay conscious of these things, we continue to work the program to the best of our ability every day, in all our affairs. It also helps us see that all we have gone through wasn't bad if we can turn it around and use it for good. It is an amazing feeling to be able to use our life experiences, beliefs, spirituality, to make a difference in another person's life.

Recovery is like love. You can't keep it unless you give it away. We won't have to go out and seek others who need our help. When we are living in spirituality, turning things over to a God of our understanding on a daily basis, those people will be put in our path. Our job is to recognize the opportunity and take action.

We will come to believe there are no accidents when we are living right with ourselves and God. With every new situation, there is something to be learned, and with every person we meet, there is an exchange that needs to take place. It might not seem terribly important as we walk down the street to smile at a stranger, to wish someone a good morning, or just to open the door for another person. However, these things are important.

There are times when all of us have been down, when we wonder what it's all about, when life doesn't seem that great. People get lost, and feel a disconnection to the world around them. It is astounding the difference a small gesture can make. I've heard that the best thing you can say to someone who is considering taking their own life is that you would miss them. It seems so little, but it means so much that one other person cares if they fall off the face of the Earth. It can make a difference.

These are the things that keep us out of ego: considering the feelings and needs of others, respecting their rights to live their lives, to believe what they believe, and knowing that this God of our understanding knows his business and doesn't need us second-guessing him. That's what true faith is about. We leave God and others to their business, and we stay in ours. That's what using a twelve-step program on a daily basis means.

Therefore, when we begin putting unrealistic expectations on others, finding ourselves feeling anger and resentments, unable to be compassionate and tolerant, we know we are slipping back into ego. We have begun that all too familiar slide into edging God out. It's a slippery slide, and at the bottom we will find the same thing we knew before . . . unhappiness. And, the wall of clutter that we hid behind will become the same prison that we fought so hard to dismantle.

We are all a part of one group . . . humanity. Pay attention and it will become clear when, where, and how you can be involved in the world. Listen to your instincts, do the next right thing for you, and leave the results to the God of your understanding. You will touch many lives you might never know about, then they will touch another life, and on and on. Like ripples in water, you never know how far it will go. You may not be able to solve all the world's problems, but you will make a difference in your own life and the lives of others.

Ego, total self-involvement, will take a person back to addiction faster than any other thing. That's why the last three steps of a twelve-step program are essential.

They are the steps that help us maintain a better way of life, keep us alert to the signs that we are edging God out, that we are in danger of repeating behaviors that can only end one way.

Get involved in humanity. Let go of expectations, and you will never be disappointed. Live in the truth, and know that as long as you are right with yourself and the God of your understanding, it will be okay. Open yourself to the world, and the world will open itself to you. You will never feel the need to hide behind that wall of clutter again.

The Inspired Life

Sought through prayer and meditation to improve our conscious contact with God, as we understood God, praying only for the knowledge of God's will for us and the power to carry that out.

STEP 11, "Sought through prayer and meditation to improve our conscious contact with God, as we understood God, praying only for the knowledge of God's will for us and the power to carry that out," is how we come to live an inspired life.

There are three facets to Step 11. We seek. We improve. We become stronger.

It is a human trait to be a seeker. There are times in our lives that we seek avoidance and escape. During those times, we pull toward addictions. The addictions take over and become our life. That's when we become unhappy, unfulfilled people, caught up in a web of our own making. Feelings of hopelessness, and helplessness, can set in.

We seek a way out. In fact, we may try many ways out, believing it should be within our power to fix. However, for those of us who are true addicts, it's like trying to control diarrhea with willpower.

We seek answers through others who have suffered our addiction and have come out on the other side. At that point, we are faced with a twelve-step program.

It's not easy, but we work hard at the steps, and with time, things get better. By the time we reach Step 11, we've discovered some answers. We've resolved past issues, made amends, found a God of our understanding, and have developed a program that works for us. The feelings of hopelessness and helplessness disappear. We have come to understand what it is to know serenity, even happiness. However, Step 11 tells us we are not finished.

We have embarked upon a spiritual journey, one day at a time, for a lifetime. The step says that through prayer and meditation we will "improve" our conscious contact with the God of our understanding. It's been said that we are spiritual beings having a physical experience. If that's true, then it is time to become a spiritual seeker, to open ourselves to the answers to the life the God of our understanding wants for us.

Even though we are in recovery, life keeps happening. People we care about may get ill, some will die, we may suffer from disease, heartache, disappointments, and a myriad of other human experiences and feelings. It's all part of the physical experience. What we do with those things, with our life, with the way we think, is the spiritual experience.

When we are praying only for knowledge of God's will for us, and the power to carry that out, and listening through meditation, we will know that whatever happens, it will be okay. If we honestly believe that the essence of who we are, or the spirit, will live on, our perception, not only of death, but of life will change.

Life stops being good and bad, and becomes a series of experiences that teach us and show us the way. We will know that it's okay to be a happy, serene person even when seemingly bad things happen. There is a difference between thinking and knowing. When faith grows, becomes stronger, there is a knowing deep within us.

The big question is, how do we know what God's will for us is? As addicts, desperate for control, we live on self-will run riot. Our instinct, that gut level part of us that tells us what to do, has failed us time and again, taking us to that point when we are pleading with a higher power to intervene. How is God to speak to us but through the very same instincts? The mind? We must watch out for the mind. It can fool us into believing what we want to believe, can lead us astray, but the soul will never deceive us. It is a leap of faith, and takes practice to learn to trust our instincts, but when we are right with the God of our understanding, living our lives to the best of our ability, and know we are responsible for every choice in our lives, the truth will be revealed. When we live in truth, our instincts will never fail us.

In Step 3, we turn our will and life over to the God of our understanding each day. Step 11 takes that practice further. It brings us to God in every circumstance, with every person we meet, throughout our day. It teaches us that for every problem we encounter, whether it is an unkind thought or action toward others or ourselves, we have been endowed with the tools to correct it. When we are not sure which one to use, we ask.

We ask through prayer, and listen for answers through meditation. Meditation is nothing more than a quiet time, after prayer, to listen, to leave ourselves open to the truth. The truth of the situation will tell us what needs to be done. Many times, doing the next right thing won't be easy, won't be convenient, but if we've chosen to live a spiritual life, it is the only thing that will keep us from living in conflict with ourselves. Those who live in a state of conflict do not know serenity and peace.

For instance, after a number of years of recovery, I had the opportunity to start my own business. It was something I'd secretly dreamed of for years. The business thrived. I found an organization that was devoted to businesses of this type, that held conventions for members of the organization. Thrilled to be a part of it all, I joined.

After a few years, I began to notice things in the organization that bothered me. At first, they were little things that I could rationalize and justify. I let them pass because I loved going to the conventions, the new friends I had so much in common with, and the excitement. Soon I was faced with a situation I could no longer ignore. I stewed about it, I thought about it, and finally I went to my hotel room and prayed about it. I knew all along what the right thing to do was, but if I did it, this would be my last convention.

I returned to the convention and spoke up, in a rational manner, about the situation, and resigned. I didn't point fingers, place blame on any one person, get into a self-righteous tirade. I simply confronted what was happening to hurt myself and others in the organization, and I removed myself from it. Even though I wasn't the one wronging others, if I stayed, if I continued to make excuses because I didn't want to give up something, I would have been in the wrong. I would have continually had to bite my tongue and suppress all those emotions I'd been feeling. I would have been in conflict with myself, and with the God of my understanding.

Many years later, after I became an author, I was asked to attend the convention as a speaker, a teacher, and to sign books I'd written on the subject. God had not only shown me the way, given me the strength to do what needed to be done, but I was led down a new path and was given closure.

That may not seem like a big life decision, but I've come to believe that all the decisions we make are important. The myriad of choices we make each day determines who we are and how we live our life. We ask, we listen, we act by doing the next right thing, even though it may be difficult at the moment, and we discover what it is to live in truth, to understand what God's will for us is.

I've been told that when it is right, all the doors will open, and if it's not, no matter what we do, they will remain closed. There is an old adage that says if you have to break down walls and walk over broken glass to get where you're going, that's probably not where you need to be. Life just shouldn't be that hard. However, for many people, who think they can make their lives happen, it is. There is the life we think we should live, and the one God has for us. It stands to reason that once we've discovered the right path, life will be better. It will be easier simply because we aren't traveling alone.

If we make a conscious effort every day to connect, in everything, we won't worry about the results. They are out of our hands. What will be, will be, in God's time, and in God's way. I know from personal experience that God has great timing. God gives us what we need when we are ready for it.

Living an inspired life requires total surrender to the God of your understanding and the faith that no matter what happens, it will always be for your best. When you know that in the deepest core of your being, you cannot help but be an inspiration to others. God will shine through you.

Let Go and Let God

We think we have so much control over our lives. That is, until something happens to remind us that life is constant change. The harder we hold onto believing we are in control of everything, the more difficult it is to deal with those things. We may attempt to avoid the reality of the situation, or escape the fact that we are out of control, but the truth is the truth, and sooner or later it will see the light of day. For those of us who need to feel in control, that can be devastating.

You may think of an obsessive-compulsive personality trying to control the world around them. Their need for control shows in the need for perfection. Everything must be in its place, and clean. The clutter addict is like a reverse obsessive-compulsive. Everything is out of place, and not so tidy. They are saying by their actions, "It's my life, my stuff, and I can live any way I want to." It's one thing they do have control over—or at least they believe that.

The clutter addict may convince themselves, and tell others, that there's not enough time in the day, there are so many things that get in the way of what they intended to do, that they'll get things done when their life calms down a bit. However, it never seems to calm down. It may seem incongruent, but being overwhelmed is a control issue.

As long as the clutter addict is overwhelmed with things that need to be done, situations that need to be taken care of, other people they just can't deal with, they have no time, energy, or inclination to look at themselves. Their total focus is looking over the wall of clutter, outside themselves. There is no room in their thoughts to see what is really going on inside.

Even after the clutter addict finds their way to a twelve-step program, is forced through working the steps to face the addiction and face themselves, letting go and letting God can be difficult. Like most other addicts, they must be careful of extremes. Whether they are living in chaos or attempting to do everything perfectly, it's still an extreme, and still a control issue.

One of the most difficult things for an addict to do is to go with the flow of life, not trying to make life happen the way they want. It can become an exercise in frustration and disappointment that can cause a relapse in recovery. It's as if they are saying, "Look at me. I'm trying so hard. See what happened. What's the point?"

Whether we are in a twelve-step program or not, living the best life we can or not, even if we are connected to a God of our understanding, life keeps happening. No one gets immunity. Stuff happens to everyone. The difference between a happy person and an unhappy person is their perception of life and why things happen.

I used to think my life was an accident of birth. If I'd been born into a more functional family, a more affluent situation, if I'd been smarter, prettier, or had some amazing talent, my life would have been better. I certainly tried many unusual ways to have some of those things in my life. I got a taste of some of them at times, but they never lasted because they didn't belong to me.

Even after getting into a twelve-step program, it took me a while to figure out the difference between surviving life and living life. That epiphany came through learning to let go and let God.

When I was close to hungry, and homeless, I asked God to put me where I needed to be. God gave me a job I never would have sought out. It was the best thing that ever happened to me.

When a financial situation came up that I didn't think could be resolved, I asked God to show me the way. God showed me a way out. It wasn't easy, and it required a lot of extra work, but it was the solution.

When tragedy hit and I feared falling back into my addiction, I asked God to give me strength. God gave it to me through other people who loved and supported me. They showed up seemingly out of the blue.

When a relationship problem that I'd tried to deal with for years kept bothering me, I finally turned it over to the God of my understanding. A miracle happened. I was reunited with the only man I'd ever loved, the man I'd hoped to marry fifteen years earlier. We have now been married for more than twenty years.

No matter what I asked of God, there was always an answer. Granted, it was not always the answer I hoped for, or expected, but it always ended up for my best. Maybe that is the answer to the peace and serenity I got through letting go and letting God—no expectations.

Life is a series of choices, but we don't have to make them alone. If we ask this God of our understanding for a solution, an answer, and God puts it in front of us, who are we to argue? Obviously, what we've been doing with our life hasn't worked, or we wouldn't be asking for help.

As a human being, attempting to control my own life, I didn't have a clue. However, whenever I let go and let God, and pay attention, the solutions are clear. I said they were clear, but not always easy. Some of the most difficult solutions have been the most rewarding. There's something to be said for taking God's hand and walking through the fears that keep us from living life.

These days, every time I think my life can't get any better, it does. When I learned to let go, and let God guide my life, doors opened that I couldn't have dreamed of in my wildest imagination. Every secret desire I had tucked away deep within, because I didn't dare say them out loud, has been given to me through the grace of God.

I found hope through a twelve-step meeting, listening to others like me who discovered that through a God of their understanding, they would have the life God planned for them, a life full of purpose. That is, if they were willing to let go, and let God.

Step 12

Pass It On

Having had a spiritual awakening as a result of these steps, we tried to carry this message to others, and to practice these principles in all our affairs.

STEP 12, "Having had a spiritual awakening as a result of these steps, we tried to carry this message to others, and to practice these principles in all our affairs," has to do with giving back that which we were so freely given.

Have you ever gone to a doctor, some thin, young person, who is probably able to eat anything she desires without gaining a pound, and tried to discuss diet? Would you consider having a straightforward talk about sex with a priest or nun who had never had sex? They may have wonderful insights to share with you about many things, but they cannot understand your immediate frustrations because they have never lived through your experience.

By working a twelve-step program devoted to your clutter addiction, you are uniquely qualified to work with other clutter addicts. By the time you reach Step 12, your life will have gone through many drastic changes, not only in the way you live, but in your belief system. Others will notice the changes and may wonder how you did it.

If you have vigorously worked the steps, are walking your talk, you will be a living example of hope for the still-suffering clutter addict. However, you must remember that you can't give it away if you don't have it. You can only speak from where you've been.

What is it you must have? An uncluttered house? That's not enough. Many clutter addicts can get their house cleaned up and cleared out for periods of time. You must have an uncluttered life, one based in spirituality. Just like the uncluttered house reflects how you live, the uncluttered life is reflected in who you are every day, in every way.

You don't have to be perfect, but you do need to strive for progress in your program, in your life. No one will ever live the perfect life, or work a perfect program. You are human, after all. And, that's all right. Your accept-ance of imperfection, as humbling as it may be, will be of help in working with others. It would be daunting for a newcomer to feel as if you are on a level they could never reach. Instead of giving hope, you might over-whelm them even more.

Where will these others come from? They may find you through an online meeting, a regular meeting, hear about you from a third party, or be a friend or relative. You will be amazed at some of the people who seek you out. Clutter addicts come from all walks of life, from all economic levels. The addiction is no respecter of age, gender, or race.

Does the still-suffering clutter addict find you by acci-dent? I don't think so. I believe that two people are brought together through divine intervention, at the right time for both of them. It's as important for the person who is helping as it is for the person being helped.

How do you help? At first, in your enthusiasm to share what you have, you must be careful not to become a caretaker, not to try to do it for the other person. No one could do it for you, and you can't do it for them. Your job is to plant the seed of hope, but it will grow in God's time.

You must go into this helping with compassion, tolerance, patience, and most of all, no expectations. They are not doing this for you, or on your timetable. You can provide reassurance that the steps are suggested, and that if, and when, they are ready to tackle one, you are willing to share your experience. You are available to them when the need arises.

You are not there to bail addicts out financially, but perhaps to tell them how you resolved your financial problems, and how long it took. You are not there to clean their house, but to allow them to remove their wall of clutter when they are ready. You are not there to solve family problems, but to make suggestions that within the steps, they might find the answer. You may suggest outside counseling. You are not their parent, their guru, their therapist. You will not make decisions for them, or tell them what they have to do, or when. The most effective words are, "When I was in that situation, I did (whatever you did that worked for you). You might try praying about it." You are there to encourage them to find their own answers, and if your experience, strength, and hope can help, all the better.

There may be times you will need to guide the new-comer to another person. They may be living through an experience you have yet to encounter. You cannot tell another person what you did if you didn't do it. You can't imagine what you would do in the situation. If you know people in the program, have listened to their stories, perhaps you know someone who has experienced something similar. Get your ego out of the way, and introduce them. Whether someone gets into recovery from clutter addiction is not about making yourself look good as a helper, but about their choices. In some cases, you can give it your best shot, but they are simply not ready. Even then, you have not failed. You planted the seed. It may not grow right away, or even for some time, but it is there and will grow when it's time.

If you are wondering what to say to a newcomer, when they are ready, you can't say anything wrong, and when they are not, you can't say anything right. If you speak your truth, based on what you did in the program, it can't be wrong.

You may feel reluctant to talk to the newcomer about God for fear of scaring them off. Take the time while they are still on their first step, to get to know the person, a bit of their background, whatever they are willing to share, and wait until they are ready for the second step to get into the spiritual aspect of the program. Help them to realize that it is a God of their understanding. If they are not yet ready to accept a God of their understanding, or a God of anyone's understanding, they can give thought to a Higher Power. In the beginning, they may use the Clutterers Anonymous group as a power greater than themselves. Spirituality, like every other part of the program, must come to every person in their own time, in their own way.

When I think of working with others, passing it on, I think of one young lady I worked with for years. She came into the twelve-step program as a young, unmarried mother, with little or no education, and suffering from several addictions. We talked. I chose to help her if I could. There were times she asked me things, and I gave her my honest opinion as taken from my own life experiences, and she got angry. Each time, I backed off until she contacted me again. I watched her struggle, just as I had, with each new step. I shared what I could when she would allow it. Otherwise, I left her alone with her choices.

Many traumatic events happened even after she got into recovery, but this young woman held onto the program, the people in the program, without returning to her addictions. Things got better, but were not always easier for her. Still, she hung in there with the hope that she'd finally found something that might work. It was working for others.

One day, I looked at her and knew something had changed. There was a new confidence about her, a smile that looked as if she'd discovered a secret. Yes, she'd had a spiritual breakthrough. When that awakening happened, it was as if suddenly she got it. It all made sense. She not only awakened to a God of her understanding, but to life. That's what Step 12 says: you will have a spiritual awakening "as a result of these steps."

Once the connection was made to a God of her understanding, with direction from the steps in the program and the support of others, her new life began. She worked hard, accepted help when needed, and the person she truly was, the one before the addictions overtook her, emerged. Today, she has a real life. It's a life filled with family, friends, a job working with other addicts, and is happy, joyous, and free. She has come to be the daughter I never had. And, she is a walking example of hope. She has touched many lives, including my own.

It is a wonderful feeling to watch a miracle happen, to feel as if you were even a small part of it. It gives you a feeling of purpose. It helps you know that all those things you went through, that struggle through the steps, might actually make a difference, not only in your life, but in the lives of others.

As you grow in the twelve-step program, begin to work with others who suffer from the same addiction, there will be a discovery that might surprise you. As you practice the principles, they begin to spill out into the rest of your life, to your other relationships. Each day becomes a new experience, wondering what the God of your understanding has in store for you.

As you walk through each fear, your spirituality gets stronger, and you get stronger within yourself. Your steps will get lighter, and you may find yourself smiling for no reason at all. The past will no longer haunt you, your dreams, or affect your relationships. In fact, you will find that your past experiences help you relate to, and help, others. You will feel a sense of purpose in your life. There will be a clarity and focus that you have never known before. Fear slips away as you believe that no matter what happens, as long as you have a God of your understanding in your corner, you will intuitively know how to handle it. You will know it's okay to be happy, to feel that serenity, even when seemingly bad things are happening around you. There will be a realization that the God of your understanding is doing for you what you could not do for yourself.

It may not all happen at once, but if you are rigorous in working the twelve steps to the best of your ability, and putting your trust in the One who loves you completely, you will see all these things come to pass. When they come to pass, you will have something beautiful to pass on to others. There will always be enough. The love of self and others will dismantle the wall of clutter, the clutter of the mind, that you hid your light behind. Your light will shine for all the world to see.

The Serenity Prayer

God, grant me the serenity,
to accept the things I cannot change,
the courage to change the things I can,
and, the wisdom to know the difference.

It's not through acceptance, courage, and wisdom, that we are given serenity. Serenity is ours for the asking. Grant means to give, to endow. Therefore, when we are ready for a serene life, we ask the God of our understanding to grant it to us.

Does that seem too easy? For the clutter addict, it means giving up the chaos, the excuse of always being overwhelmed. It's about burning a bridge. It's a big step, because once they say the words, there may be no going back to those old familiar, safe, clutter walls.

The clutter addict is like a butterfly. They have two choices. They can stay safely folded up in that cocoon, spend their entire life there, or they can make the efforts it takes to break free. It will be a new world, a bit frightening at first. However, that feeling of sun on them, the wind blowing them this way and that, new foods, other people trying to find their way, can be an exhilarating experience.

The effort to break free is about the steps, and a willingness to accept a God of their understanding as their life guide. With each step they take, the cocoon opens a bit more, and they become stronger. The final decision is whether to leave the cocoon for good, to step out into life with all its ups and downs, and ask to be granted the serenity needed to live a real life.

Serenity means peacefulness. Being peaceful means that when all around you chaos reigns, you know that through using the tools you have been given in a twelve-step program and the God of your understanding, everything will be okay. It will be okay because of your faith in yourself as a product of something wonderful. It will be okay because you have come to understand that life doesn't end here, that you are here to experience every part of this human existence, and to learn.

Once you have accepted the gift of serenity, you will know what it means to live in acceptance of those things you cannot change. As much as you might think you know what's best for another human being, you don't. That is between them and the God of their understanding. When you truly love someone, you allow them to travel their own path, make their own decisions, and love them no matter what.

When you understand what it took to get you where you are, even though it may have been a great struggle, you'll see that everyone has their own struggles, which ultimately take them where they need to be. You can't change another person any more than they could have changed you. The best you can do is to change your perception of others. If you stop trying to change them, stop putting expectations on them, you will immediately eliminate those feelings of anger, disappointment, and frustration. You might even get to know the person, the real person, and find them to be a unique, interesting individual.

There are many situations over which you will have no control. Besides other people, there will be things like job loss, illness, deaths, unexpected financial problems, even crime. If you have chosen to step out from behind the wall of clutter, to stop hiding in a cluttered mind, then you will have to accept that all these things

are a part of life, and you are not exempt. Like the butterfly, each effort you make to come out on the other
side will make you stronger.

One way to help find acceptance is to change your
perception. Another way is to tell yourself that, no matter what happens, it's not the end of the world. This too
shall pass. It's amazing, but time is a great healer when
you allow the healing to happen.

When my oldest son, who was the only person in my
life I'd allowed myself to care for in years, was killed, I
thought my life was over. The pain was so big, it was like
a tangible thing living inside me. I experienced crazy
thoughts. I would take poison and throw myself across
his grave to die so that everyone would know how much
I loved him and how much pain I was in. I pulled further
into my addictions and my self-destructive lifestyle. I held
onto that pain as if it were the last breath in my body.
As long as I had the pain, I never had to accept that he
was gone.

Even after I found a twelve-step program, the pain
lived on. I'd lived with that pain so long, I wasn't sure I
could exist without it. If I ever wanted to return to my
addictions, I was holding on to the perfect excuse. Slowly,
as I worked the steps, found a God of my understanding, and became willing to ask for that serenity, I changed.

I accepted not only that he was gone, but that I was here, still alive, and it was time to make a decision about how I wanted to live what was left of my life.

Today, I know that my son had completed his tasks here, and it was time for him to move on. I'm not finished. I'm not sure what I'm supposed to do, but I do know that as long as I keep a daily contact with the God of my understanding, asking for his guidance, and accept it, that my purpose here will be fulfilled. When it is, like my son, I will move on. I miss having him in my life, but I accepted the serenity so that I might live a peaceful life.

There are many things we can change, but it takes courage. Fear of the unknown is what keeps us from change. However, faith trumps fear if it's strong enough. Courage doesn't mean we have no fear, but that we are willing to walk through the fear. That willingness comes because we are no longer walking alone.

If you are in an abusive relationship, a job that wears you down and makes you unhappy, a physical problem that can be solved by medication or surgery, or simply diet and exercise, or you're living in a place you hate to go home to, whether it's a mansion or a one-room apartment, you do have choices.

Are you saying to yourself that the present situation may not be good, but what if I let it go, try something new, and it's worse? What if this is as good as it gets? What's going to happen? What if I don't deserve any better? Those are fear-based questions that will keep you from change.

What if, instead, you told yourself things based in faith, such as,

God wants me to be happy. I deserve to be happy as much as anyone else.

I am a part of God's plan, and this isn't working for me.

No matter where I go, who I'm with, what job I'm doing, where I live, as long as I'm true to myself, to my God, I will know serenity.

God is my guide, and he will lead where I need to be and put me with the people I need to be with.

No matter what happens, it's always for my best. It's better to struggle for freedom and happiness than to accept misery.

I believe the God of my understanding wants me to have the best life I can, to thrive and be happy, joyous, and free. When I live that way, I can offer hope to the hopeless, help to the helpless, with love, compassion, and understanding. For me, that's what life is about. The happier I am, the more serenity I feel, the more I can live in peace, no matter what's going on around me, and the more I have to give to others. The more I give away, the more I have.

Each step you take will take courage, but the end results will be worth the effort. If it's an unacceptable situation and you have the power to change it, and you don't, there is no one to blame but you. You can't cry about the life God gave you when he also gave you the ability to choose, to change.

It's too easy to say that this is your lot in life and there's nothing you can do about it. Therein lies the wisdom to know the difference. Whether you wish to admit it or not, even if you have a gun pointed at your head, you have a choice to comply or to die.

Other people will be who they are, death and illness will come, jobs may end abruptly, and finances may go up and down no matter what you do. The wise know that these things are out of their control, but what they do with them is not. If situations are handled with acceptance, then, and only then, can they move on with faith that there is a reason for everything.

Have you ever gotten into a relationship with another person, and suddenly, something isn't right? All of a sudden, you cringe when the phone rings, or when you encounter them at a social gathering, you find yourself hiding or leaving? You may not be able to change the person, but you can certainly change whether or not you spend time with them. You have the option to be honest and move on. When you have the courage to do so, you will know that new freedom of the butterfly just released from its cocoon.

We can feel really helpless when facing illness. It's difficult to imagine what good could come from being sick. However, a serious illness can help us put things in perspective. All those little life dramas don't seem nearly as important. Money, and possessions, have lost their appeal. We look around at others, listen to them bicker over petty things, and think how unimportant those things are. If that's the worst thing they have to worry about, those people are in good shape.

The wise take that experience, what they learned about what is important in their life, because of their illness or the illness of someone they love, and hold onto it. They will have learned the value of life, health, having another day with someone they love. They may not have been able to change what was going on with the illness, but the illness has changed their perception.

Death is devastating, many times even if we don't know the person. We hear about a child dying, and it makes our heart hurt. Perhaps the child fell into an un-gated pool and drowned. We have absolutely no control over what happened, but the situation may cause us to watch our children closer, to replace the broken gate on the fence around the pool, or to teach our child to swim. The wise learn not only from their mistakes but from the mistakes of others.

When someone we love dies, after we've grieved, we can go one of two ways. We can hold onto the pain throughout our life, allowing it to affect us in so many ways, in fear of loving completely again, or we can learn how precious life, and love, are, how fortunate we were to have love in our life, and that it was worth all the pain. The wise honor the relationship they had with the person they lost, by loving again with the same vigor. They do not waste precious days, and moments, that can never be relived.

Jobs and money are a big deal to many. After all, we may be spiritual beings, but we have to live on this Earth, and that requires food, shelter, and housing. It's highly unlikely we are going to get them without work and money.

A job is what you do to earn money to exchange for goods. It's wonderful if you like what you're doing, if you've made a career out of your job. What would happen if, without warning, the business closed, or downsized, and you lost your job? For some, this is as serious as a death.

If you can remind yourself of the difference between who you are and what you do, and place your faith in a God of your understanding, you will find acceptance that perhaps there is someplace else you need to be, or something else you need to do.

After getting into recovery, establishing a business that I loved, that was thriving, I got sick. It took me a while to come to the acceptance that I would no longer be able to take care of my business. I went through all the stages of mourning.

I felt like God had jerked the rug out from under me. In denial, I continued to work until I nearly killed myself. In anger, I railed against God and the illness. I stopped working the program, I refused to pray, to listen, to believe, because things weren't going the way I wanted them to, the way I had expected them to.

It wasn't until I found acceptance that I could begin healing, physically and spiritually. I finally surrendered myself to the God of my understanding, and continued to do that on a daily basis. With God's help, and the help of those who cared for me, I went through treatment, surgeries, and several years of recovery, and came to believe that whatever happened, it would be okay. Even if I died, I'd had a wonderful second chance in life, had lived it well, and for the first time in my life, was a happy human being. What more could one ask?

During my recovery, I began to write. My husband and I went to Arizona to visit my brother. Since a lot of my tragedy had occurred in Arizona, I once swore I would never return there. But, there I was in this little mountain community. Within a few months, we'd sold our businesses, moved to that small town, and I'd become an author.

It seemed God had a plan for me, and it took everything it took to get me here doing what I'm doing today. It took the wisdom to understand that the change in my life wasn't to punish me, to take anything from me, but to lead me to my destiny.

It's been said that when we cease fighting everything, and everyone, we discover the life we are meant to live. When I think of that, I always consider the birds and animals. Instinctively, they follow their lives. They seem to know where to go, when, and how to survive. They concern themselves with each day, not worrying about the past or future. Ah, that we could live so instinctively. However, we are humans, endowed with a different consciousness. And the wisdom to know the difference is part of that consciousness.

Wisdom comes not only from our personal experiences, but from other's experiences. We can look at a burn scar on someone else and know that it was a painful experience. There is no need for us to set ourselves on fire. Life is one learning experience after another, and we will know wisdom when, and if, we are open to it.

The twelve steps are the process by which we find the truth, a direction to go, and later, the wisdom not to repeat our past transgressions. That is the road to wisdom, one step at a time. What are these wisdoms?

Step 1   Clutter is affecting my life.

Step 2   I am not insane.

Step 3   I am not alone.

Step 4   I know what I did.

Step 5   If it's not a secret, it can't hurt me.

Step 6   God will help me remove my defects.

Step 7   All I have to do is ask God.

Step 8   I can become willing.

Step 9   I can make amends.

Step 10   I can live better today.

Step 11   God will show me the way.

Step 12   My experience can help others.

The wisdom to know the difference tells us that if we are paying attention, working our steps, turning our will and life over to the God of our understanding, and have ceased fighting everything and everyone that we can't change. By changing those things that have kept us unhappy, we will discover the life we were meant to live. We will be that butterfly, free and unfettered from that clutter cocoon.

Happy, Joyous, and Free

In your formative years, those people closest to you teach you what it is to be happy. Once grown, your peers take over, and throughout your life, society tells you, in so many ways, what it takes to be happy.

Parents tend to go one of two ways. If they are unhappy or unfulfilled in their lives, they may attempt to teach you how to avoid the problems they experienced. If they have been happy, they may decide that what made them happy will make you happy, and try to form you into that mold.

Your friends' attitudes are a result of those people who are closest to them. They will either embrace their ideas or revolt against them. Either way, there has been an effect on them, just as much as there has on you.

Through advertising, movies, magazines, society tells you what you need to be happy. The cosmetic industry tells you that if you look better, you will feel better. The diet industry lets you know what you should weigh, how your body should look, and how to get there.

Movies and magazines dwell on drama, because that's what sells their products. Through all these things, and the people involved in your life, expectations are born.

Other people, according to their role in your life, are expected to act in certain ways. You may have expectations of how your life should have progressed. When those things don't occur, or happen in a different way, the result can be not only unhappiness, but anger and resentments. Self-pity and jealousy can set in. You may become intolerant of others, of life in general. Thus begins the fear that brings on the clutter walls.

The search for happiness begins. At first, things can make you happy, but like any other addiction, the fix only lasts a short time, and you will need another. The allure of possessions is that they are what they are. You either like them or not. You don't have to worry about complexities, like you would with other people. You know exactly what to expect with a thing. If you don't get what you expect, you can simply discard it. It's not that easy with other human beings.

If you want to be happy, the answer will come through freedom. A twelve-step program can not only give you freedom from the clutter, but from fear of living life, dealing with other people, and taking risks. Only the first step of the program mentions clutter. The rest of the steps tell you how to live an uncluttered life. If you work the steps, one of the greatest lessons you will learn is that you don't owe anybody anything, any more, and they don't owe you anything. The expectations are removed. It frees you in a way you may never have experienced before.

It's almost like starting life over again through the eyes of a child. You can free that child within that really does want to be a part of things, play with the other kids, be open and trusting. You will begin to feel joy in the smallest things: a smile, a kind gesture, doing something for another with no expectations, surrounding yourself with beauty and harmony, embracing life on life's terms, each day a lifetime to be lived out to the fullest. These are the things that will make you happy.

Happiness is not a set of circumstances and cannot be found in possessions. It is a feeling that you carry with you into your life each day. You have a choice to be happy or unhappy each day. Joy is a result of happiness. When you are joyous, you can't help but be a joy to others. Both of these things are a result of freeing yourself, and a twelve-step program can show you the way.

If you choose to work the twelve steps of Clutterers Anonymous, understand that it is not a quick fix, but a way of life, and you have the rest of your life to work the steps, one day at a time. Read through the steps. There is nothing there that can hurt you. In fact, if you are able to work them, they are bound to make your life better.

The twelve steps of Clutterers Anonymous can set you free from the past, from fears, from feeling separate from your fellows, from expectations. You can be happy, joyous, and free.

Affirmations

I deserve to live in serenity, in my house, and in my mind.

I am never alone as long as I have a God of my understanding and my support group. I have but to ask.

I have been endowed by God, and empowered by the twelve steps, with all the tools I need to handle any situation.

I don't compare myself, my life, to others.

I no longer need to make excuses for myself. I am a product of something wonderful.

Time is my friend, not my enemy.

When I feel overwhelmed, I can stop, pray, and eliminate whatever is not needed until I find a livable place for me.

Every choice I make, each day, is important because it defines my character.

When I pray, I am shown the way.

Nothing is bad if I learn from it.

God brings the people I need in my life each day. I can choose to trust.

I have no expectations of others. I accept them as
   they are.
I know the importance of balance in work, rest,
   and recreating.
I can focus, without getting distracted, on one task
   at a time.
I do not have to be perfect, but strive for progress on a
   daily basis.
I have reasonable goals, and finish one project before
   beginning another.
My work does not define me. It's what I do, not who I am.
The God of my understanding may have different plans
   for me than I have. I can be flexible.
I am an inspiration simply because I walk my talk, and
   live a better life.
My experience, strength, and hope can help others.
Every moment, every person, counts.
When I live in the God of my understanding's will for
   me, whatever I have is enough.
Possessions, and pets, cannot replace intimate relation-
   ships with people.
I am kind to myself because I deserve it.
I have the rest of my life to work the twelve steps of
   Clutterers Anonymous. I don't have to do it all
   today.